PIETRO ARCHIATI (1944-2022) was born near Brescia in Italy. From the age of ten he attended a monastery school in a small missionary Order. After graduating from high school, he studied theology and philosophy in Rome and Munich. He worked in Laos as a teacher during the Vietnam War and later as a missionary in New York, including in the Marriage Encounter movement. In 1977, while a hermit on Lake Como in Italy, he discovered anthroposophy, which became his lifelong passion. He later said: 'Within days… I knew with profound certainty: This is what you have been looking for your whole life… Its effect on me was like a hurricane.' From 1981 he worked in South Africa as a lecturer in a seminary. Tension with the Church increased with time and ultimately led to his work no longer being possible within its framework. After leaving the Church in 1987, he became a freelance speaker and an author of numerous books. From 2004 until his death, he co-founded a publishing company, Rudolf Steiner Ausgaben. His many prefaces and epilogues to the Steiner volumes he published are an attempt to build a bridge between anthroposophy and contemporary life.

# LOVE

*The Mysterious Logic of the Heart*

Pietro Archiati

Translated by Paul King

TEMPLE LODGE

Temple Lodge Publishing Ltd.
Hillside House, The Square
Forest Row, RH18 5ES

www.templelodge.com

First published in English by Temple Lodge Publishing, 2025

Originally published in German under the title *Das Geheimnis der Liebe, Die Logik des Herzens ist anders* by Rudolf Steiner Ausgaben, Bad Liebenzell, in 2003

This translation © Temple Lodge Publishing 2025



A CIP catalogue record for this book is available from the British Library

ISBN 978 1 915776 28 0

Cover by Morgan Creative
Typeset by Symbiosys Technologies, Visakhapatnam, India
Printed by 4Edge Ltd., Essex

# Contents

# Foreword

It is not easy at this time to be so brazen as to write yet another book about love. The word *love* has become so hackneyed that it can mean almost everything and nothing. But it was precisely for that reason that I felt challenged to write this book nevertheless, because despite everything, I am convinced that there are still very many people who want to learn more about love because for them it is the most important thing in life. But even though there are many who feel this way, there are still not enough, and I should think myself lucky if due to this book the number increased by even just one more person.

For those who are reading one of my books for the first time, I should not wish to fail to mention that for everything I have to say and write about I owe the deepest debt of gratitude to one individual in particular: Rudolf Steiner. Without him many of the thoughts expressed here about love would not have been written. Furthermore I must confess that my opinion of the hotly controversial topic of sexuality has changed a good deal since I have tried to see it in a broader context of development. Because this subject is so controversial, the decision to engage with it was at the same time a decision to risk arousing strong opposition in many readers. I could perhaps have avoided this subject if I did not consider all it contains to be of vital importance for modern humanity.

The thoughts in this book have my mother to thank for their origin, for whose loving heart they seemed as natural as the sun, the earth, and her ten peasant children. I have written these pages from inner conversation with her. Although I naturally regard what I write to be correct or true, it is not my main concern to proclaim absolute truths, especially since these do not exist. What is most important for me is to stimulate the reader not simply to accept what I write but to test it with their own thinking. What conclusions they then come to with their own thinking is to a certain extent a matter only for themselves. I am only interested in contributing to the art of thinking becoming ever more imaginative for them, because I am convinced that this is the best way for everyone to make progress in their search for truth. I would therefore hope not so much for readers who are of my opinion or of a different one, but rather for readers who add a thousand new thoughts of their own to mine.

I hope these pages will be of use to all those who have always known that what our world needs most of all today is love, and that it is love that people need most urgently today because the deepest—albeit often unacknowledged—human longing of our time is the longing for true love.

*Pietro Archiati, Autumn 2003*

# 1. Love and Hate

## *The Salt and Pepper of Life*

## Everything begins with sympathy and antipathy

There are two feelings that accompany us throughout our life. Wherever we go, whoever we meet, whatever new and surprising events occur—these things always arouse sympathy and antipathy in us. Nothing can stop this. There is no work, no relationship, no intention that is free of them. And they are not without effect: they change things, drive them along, and can create a lot of confusion. Sympathy and antipathy are like the salt and pepper of life. They are opposites between which the path of human life meanders. Likings and dislikings determine the course of life's development. The cool, calculating intellect is often at a loss as to how to deal with them, and would really rather they didn't keep interfering all the time.

It is certainly worth the effort to go more deeply into these forces, to try to get a deeper understanding of the two fundamental feelings that determine our behaviour in all our encounters and in all the events of our lives.

We do the nature of these forces an injustice if we regard them from the outset as simply good or bad. The fact that someone experiences sympathy or antipathy cannot in itself be good or bad. A person is not responsible for the fact that these feelings arise in them, but they *are* responsible for how they deal with them, for how they outwardly express their feelings, how they act based on these feelings. It is in our nature that we are ceaselessly pervaded by all sorts of feelings and emotions, each one of us in their own way since no one can have exactly the same mix of liking and disliking as someone else.

We can look at two extreme examples: at being in love, and at a strong aversion to someone. The feeling of being in love is almost the most irresistible thing a person can experience. They are smitten by this feeling completely, it overcomes them, it literally runs away with them without their being able to do anything about it. We are no less defenceless against a violent feeling of dislike. When we detest someone, they simply repel us whether we like it or not, and we can't help but try to avoid them as much as possible.

All experiences of sympathy and antipathy arise from two sources, from two inner forces that can be called *love* and *hate*. But we must be clear what we mean here by these two words. The word 'hate' is put here in inverted commas to designate everything that a person spontaneously rejects or has to reject, everything they rightly spurn, that they wish to keep away from themselves or those they love because they fear it could harm them.

Something similar applies to the word 'love'. Every experience of sympathy is an expression of the force of love in the human being. The word *love* must also not be taken in a limited sense because love cannot isolate itself from any other force. It encompasses everything a person experiences or undergoes inwardly. This is precisely what makes an examination of love so difficult, particularly for a scientifically trained person who is used to looking at the object of their research within strictly defined boundaries. To do this in relation to love, however, would mean to exclude its deeper nature right from the outset.


## Can hate harm love?

Many think that hate is the opposite of love. But is this really the case? Do love and hate really relate to each other like two mutually excluding opposites? Do they relate like, for example, courage and cowardice, cheerfulness and sorrow, light and darkness—where each drives back the other? If this were the case, the more we loved, the less we would hate, and the more we hated, the less we would love. But this is not how things are as we can easily see by taking a closer look.

The world is full of people who assert they love one person more than anything, and hate someone else from the bottom of their soul. The liking we extend to one person does not inevitably diminish the dislike we feel towards someone else. In the case of moods, the situation is completely different. Happiness seems to steep the whole world in a bright light; when we are sad, everything seems grey. Cheerfulness drives out sadness and vice versa. But love doesn't prevent hate, and hate likewise can never drive out love.

What conclusion can we draw from this? If it is true that opposites exclude each other, and no less true that love and hate cannot mutually exclude each other, then this surely means that hate is not the opposite of love, and therefore cannot extinguish it. And if even hate cannot extinguish love, then what else could?

The reason that love knows no opposite lies in the fact that love itself is the force by which every individual ceaselessly aspires to the proper mid-point between all opposites, all one-sidedness, in life. When a person feels annoyance or even anger, it is love that arouses their perhaps unconscious longing for more equanimity, because they sense that anger doesn't get them anywhere. When someone becomes too indolent or even too lazy, they long—no matter how unconsciously—for something to stimulate them into motion once more, to help them get past their sluggishness. Love is the force that makes all one-sidedness, all deficiency, unbearable. In their one-sidedness, a person then painfully misses the other side, and this privation sooner or later sets them searching for what is missing—and what else does searching for something mean but *loving* it? Thus love is the inextinguishable longing for continuous development, the aspiration towards fulfilment, the unquenchable thirst for perfection.

Man and woman in many respects are opposites. If someone is too one-sidedly masculine, love arouses in them a longing for the feminine. To long for something, to wish for it—this is exactly what love is. What a person longs for already belongs to them because they think and seek it, and yet, on the other hand, not yet, because they still have to become it. Precisely this being *and* not being, this inexorable striving, this never-ending becoming, is the experience of love.

Let us suppose that someone has got it into their head that all the problems in life can only be solved by kindliness and giving way. Sooner or later they will have to realize from experience that through their one-sided demeanour they are always one step behind other people, that their one-track good-naturedness can harm not only themselves but others as well. It will not be long before the desire arises in them to assert themselves a little more energetically, to 'stand their ground', so as not to be constantly falling behind. If, on the other hand, someone is one-sided in always being too brash, too self-assertive, it will eventually become too much for others. These others will start to defend themselves against them and find pleasure in 'getting one over on them' from time to time. Even this individual will eventually start to wonder whether they shouldn't develop a little bit in the other direction and be somewhat more friendly towards their fellow human beings. The longing for the mid-point, the search for the balance between audacity and diffidence is nothing less than a form of love, of inner aspiration.

Love makes people inwardly mobile because being human means always being on the search for the proper balance between all the opposites of life. Love is the striving for the harmony of all our inner forces, and it prompts us always to do our best.

Someone could object here that if there is really no opposite or counter-force to love, then we would all have no alternative but to love constantly. We would be able to do nothing other than love everyone and everything, and the world would be fine. Well, of course it is not, and the fact that there is not exactly an overabundance of love in the world, that our world is not in the best condition, is plain for all to see.

If we take it that the love that exists cannot be suppressed or diminished by any counter-force, then its lack in the world will not come from an existing love having been extinguished, but from the fact that it has not even arisen in the first place. Every deficiency in love is a love not given, a failure to love. The only thing that can do anything to love is not loving, because then it does not arise at all. Love really knows no opponents, but it knows absence, it can be neglected by people again and again. But we can only speak of negligence where the chance to love has not been seized. The small amount of love that exists in humanity today can also be attributed to failures in the past, but the further development of love will depend above all on the opportunities that will be offered to humanity only in the future.

In many cases a twenty-five-year-old will certainly already have failed to perform possible acts of love, but many more opportunities to extend his love to more and more people still lie ahead of him. His lack of love is due to his omissions, but he is still at the very beginning of a long development. In this sense the whole of humanity, in terms of its consciousness, is as though in a phase of puberty. In the last few centuries, on the one hand, people have made increasingly far-reaching demands for individual freedom and love—and have thus already inevitably failed to realize a whole host of opportunities. One the other hand each individual is at the beginning of a long evolution which will still offer them many possibilities to grow in love and become more perfect.

Love is extinguished by indifference, and there is an apposite word for this: *lovelessness.* This word indicates unequivocally that something is missing—and what is missing is love. Lovelessness is the lack of affection or dislike, of sympathy or interest. It is far more difficult to overcome indifference than to assuage hatred in whatever form it might arise. As long as we hate, something is moving in us, there is life there. But if we meet the world and people with indifference, we are as good as inwardly dead. The great misery of a materialistic attitude to life results from a rampant lack of love, from a perilous lack of inner engagement. When a person does something wrong, even if they act out of hatred, they harm their development less than if they act through indifference and dullness. Dealing with indifference, finding the right therapy for it, is perhaps the most difficult thing there is.

## There is no such thing as a bit of love

Another mystery of love is the fact that is has no gradations of intensity. It can't begin slightly and become gradually stronger or vice versa. It is not like power which can become increasingly stronger, or wisdom which can become increasingly more encompassing. In love, no increase is possible: either we love another person completely and entirely, or we don't love them at all. There is no such thing as a bit of love.

Some readers might object that this is not true; most certainly there are gradations in the strength of love. 'Of course love can increase or diminish in intensity,' many will say. But is this really so? A closer look shows that what can increase are only the people or things to which our love applies. Each person can extend their love to more and more people, to more and more things. But extending love changes nothing in the nature of love itself. It is like a drop of seawater and the sea: in both cases it is exactly the same water, different only in quantity, not in quality.

Anyone can also begin to love people they didn't love before. This makes their love more encompassing, but doesn't change it in its inner nature. This is precisely why love makes us so happy: it is a power that is equally inherent in every human being, but whether a person limits it to themself or gives it to the world is a matter of their freedom. It is true that in every human being there is something like an innate desire to extend their love ever further and further, but it is like a call they are at liberty to heed, but not obliged to. This freedom concerns the occasions on which love might be shown, but not the intensity or nature of love; for these there is simply no such thing as *a bit* of love. Even though my love is just a small drop of the love that exists in the world, if I wish a person good because I love them, I will not wish them three-quarters or four-fifths of good but everything that is good for them without any deduction. This desire is either completely present in me or not at all, never just a part of it.

If a person meets ten people on a particular day, this gives the person ten opportunities to be led by their love, and if they manage it in all ten cases, they know that their behaviour towards these people was guided by love. But if they manage it only three times, it means they have omitted seven times to make love the free measure of their behaviour. If, for example, their behaviour on meeting another had been determined by fear, this does not mean that because of this there was less love in them. Love cannot determine things more or less: if it is present, it alone is the determining principle, and if it is not the determining principle, it means it is completely absent.

We can think of what often happens with young couples. For a time they have no doubt that they love each other. But at some point the day comes when perhaps the girl says to the boy, 'You don't love me any more.' She will not say: Your love has got weaker, you love me a bit less than you did. She says, 'You don't love me *any more.*' So why does she say this? Does a spontaneous statement like this correspond with reality? 'He loves me, he loves me not,' is how the old daisy game goes. . . .

The heart tells us that this is actually how it is. It asks: Do you like me or not? Do you love me or not, yes or no? It doesn't say: Let me know whether you love me ten or twenty or sixty per cent, and I will consider whether this level of your love's intensity is enough. The heart doesn't make such calculations. It sees love as indivisible, and this is what makes it such an enigma. It might perhaps make it easier to approach the mystery of love if it had some scale of measurement by which we could get our bearings, a basis of assessment, so to speak, by which we could 'measure', 'calculate', or 'weigh' love.

The example above shows that love, which for the girl was once present, can also cease. But how does this come about? If we don't use our chances to bring more and more people into the scope of our love, if we fail to notice potential circumstances to act out of love, we will love fewer and fewer people. The power to love people and the world is not rigid in any of us but dynamic by nature, and for each of us the circle of those we love becomes either larger or smaller over time. We lose interest in friends who once meant a lot to us, and the great love of previous times has now perhaps become indifferent.

When I love someone for *my own sake*, I am only interested in what I myself experience in relation to that person. I confine my love to them. Things are different when I love someone for *their sake*. In this case there is nothing else I can do but also love the people they love, the people they experience as belonging to them. In this way love constantly extends to new people. At the beginning of a love there is sympathy that arises like a gift from nature. Each individual is then free to nurture this natural liking and thus to broaden it. If it is not developed further, it remains a passion of the soul which, like all soul-life, is not lasting. The classic example for this is falling in love: just as it arises, so it also fades.

To grow in love thus means to open one's heart to ever more people and to aspire eventually to carry all people and even the whole world in one's heart. Thus the fundamental difference becomes clear between love and being 'in love'. Someone 'in love' narrows their entire attention to one single person who becomes the goal of all their wishes and longings. 'You are the only thing there is for me in the whole world,' says the lover, and naturally includes themself in this, but excludes everyone else. Real love, by its nature, inclines towards the exact opposite, to being open to all people with the most unconfined inner engagement possible, to being interested in all beings. Love is the capacity—Aristotle and Thomas Aquinas would say the 'potential'—that every individual possesses to open up in the course of their development and be interested in all people and all things. This capacity to love is laid down as predisposition in every human being without limitation. It is possible for every human being to broaden their love without limit, beyond the inclinations of their soul, since God or whoever created humankind, created no one with imperfect love.

If every human heart is such that it is able to expand its love over the whole of creation, then a person's lovelessness is all the love they have not yet given. This means, however, that the beings to whom I do not bestow my attention are those to whom I have not yet extended my love, because I have not yet sufficiently developed my own limitless potential. I could in the past perhaps have given attention to one individual or another, I could have been interested in one person or another, but I didn't do it. My lack of love corresponds to the love I have held back, that I still have to give. My indifference to human affairs never arises of itself, is never a coincidence, but it is always the result of my failures to interest myself in human beings and the world.

No one has more lovelessness in them than they themselves have caused by failing to love. No one can blame anyone else for the indifference, for the lack of love, they experience in themselves. Each of us is responsible for the richness or the poverty of our heart. If love is my innate capacity to take an interest in the deepest sense of the word in everyone and everything, and if lovelessness is what hollows me out inwardly, then love is dependent on freedom in every respect. Love is not a matter of feeling, like being 'in love', but depends entirely on the free will of each individual.

If people were compelled to love the world and everybody in it, if their capacity to love popped up willy-nilly in every situation in life, if they couldn't help but have the warmest inner involvement in everything, love would be like an urge of nature, it would not be human love. The mystery of love is inseparably bound up with freedom. Human love can only blossom where there is freedom. The only love I experience as true is the love I give in freedom. I only really love where I could also just as equally not love.

The question naturally arises here as to whether animals too can love. What is the situation, for example, with our dogs who greet us with wagging tails when we arrive home, and who, should the need arise, even defend us? Or with our cats that purr contentedly when we take them on our laps and stroke them? Whenever this question arises, there are always people only too eager to assure us that their dog or cat is most certainly capable of love, that they feel loved by their pets—and how! 'I don't know how it is with other people's pets, but *my* dog loves me, I'm quite certain of that.'

But if love is inseparably connected with free decision, then we must reconsider this question. If we are going to call animals' instinctive behaviour 'love', then we must find another word for human love.

# Three expressions of human love

Human love finds expression at three different levels corresponding to the three worlds in which the human being lives: the external world to which our *body* belongs; our purely personal, inner world, the world of the *soul* with its drives, desires, and passions; and the world of our *mind* or *spirit* in so far as the mind, using the power of thinking, is able to comprehend the world in its objective reality. The words *body, soul,* and *spirit* sound abstract to many people today, they are waiting to be filled with meaning once more. In earlier times people knew without having to think about it, what was meant by these three notions. Today it is a matter of each individual's freedom whether they exert themselves in their thinking to regain that understanding or not.

Philosophically and artistically, Greek antiquity is the basis of Western, Christian civilization. In many respects the Greek language was able to express human nature and human love more precisely than modern languages. Many people today are unable to distinguish between soul and spirit or even between body and soul. They regard inner experiences of the soul, feelings, and even ideals, as nothing more than an effect of purely physical processes—to say nothing of the spirit, which for most people today is not even worth discussing.

The ancient Greeks had three different concepts to cover the range of love's effects: *Eros* is what they called love in which the urges of nature were predominant; *philia* was feeling-love, soul-love, which expresses itself in liking, in sympathy; and *agape* was spiritual love, elective affinity, the love decided upon by each individual through free choice. Love in the sense of *agape* actually only comes to full expression with emerging Christianity, although so-called 'Platonic love' was already pointing in the same direction.

We are dealing here with three different kinds of love. Each comes to expression at a different level of life and thus has its own form of beauty. Love in all its forms of expression—at the bodily, soul, and spiritual level—can be experienced as something good.

The beauty of *Eros,* of the love rooted in the body, derives from the wisdom that inheres in all the things of nature. If the human being were purely a nature being, the question of good and evil, of what promotes human development and what hinders it, would not arise. Our ceaseless wrestling for answers only arises because the human being can really choose. We must decide for ourselves how we are going to deal with the forces of nature. Depending on how we decide, they will either serve our evolution or obstruct it. Without choice, human beings would have no freedom. And it is above all this possibility of choice that distinguishes the human being from animals. Thus it is never a natural force in itself that is good or bad for people, but solely the way of dealing with it and how this dealing works back on the human soul and spirit.

The Greek word *philia* can be translated as friendship. Its forces are not based on a natural instinct of the body like *Eros*, but on the emotional feeling of affection, of inner harmony, on the pleasure of getting on well with someone, and having the feeling of being created for each other. *Philia* also comes to expression in all our hobbies, in everything we simply like or like doing.

The beauty of spiritual love, of *agape*, is in its creative power, and presupposes our free will. This third form of love is not based on natural instinct nor is it dependant on personal sympathies. It appears when the free human spirit works creatively, when it finds a fitting word or appropriate action because it knows the beloved being well and can act accordingly out of this knowledge. It is not concerned with its own feeling experience, but solely with the flourishing of the beloved.

An example of this spiritual love is our aspiration for knowledge, since this is not determined by natural imperatives, nor does feeling play a decisive role. Someone might point out here that many people find pleasure in learning new things. They might object that we are still in the realm of *philia*, in the pleasure of the soul, and that it is impossible to speak in this case of a purely mental or spiritual love.

Think of a person who is financially secure and does not need to worry about money. If nevertheless, day in and day out, they tirelessly engage their abilities for others, although they receive neither reward nor thanks for it, and perhaps even get nothing but ingratitude—then their love is purely spiritual. It is free because it expects nothing in return. It is the love that can sometimes lead to the question: What is this for? Why am I doing this? And the simple answer can only be: Because that's how I want it! No one forces me to do it, and that is why I do it freely and out of the pure joy of doing it.

We experience our greatest happiness when we act out of a purely spiritual love of this kind. If we loved just to be happy, we would only be following our nature, since all of us long for happiness. By contrast, the free decision to act out of love is an individual deed, and happiness accompanies it mostly as a bonus, often when we least expect it. Someone who truly loves is not seeking their own happiness but that of the beloved, and therein they find their own happiness. In bodily love, by contrast, we are free only within limits since this is part of nature. It has to be, and moreover has to be as it is. Spiritual love does not have to be, it can always just as well be left undone, whereas emotional love moves to and fro between inclination towards the body and inclination towards the spirit.

## The most beautiful thing in life is love

To get closer to the mystery of love we can also look at it from the perspective of its development, for love itself is the driving force of all evolution.

We can ask: What changes has love undergone over human history? How did the Greeks love? How the Romans, the Persians, the Egyptians? What development have the forces of love undergone in Hinduism or Buddhism? What kind of love do we, who live in completely different developmental conditions, experience today? What experiences of love are possible for the first time only in our age?

If we look at love from the perspective of continuous development, we see great changes, for not all loves are equal. Even during the course of an individual life the forces of love in a ten-year-old child come to expression very differently from how they do in a fourteen-year-old boy or girl at the onset of puberty; and in a twenty-, forty-, sixty- or eighty-year-old, love reveals itself in ever new forms.

It is precisely individual biography that offers us the most beautiful opportunities for researching the transformations of the forces of love. If love is really the driving force behind all our actions and aspirations, it cannot be static or rigid. It is what always keeps us in motion, what spurs us all on to ever new development. The path of love and the path of the human being are inseparably bound together; they are two sides of the same coin.

Plato's *Symposium* is a discussion about love; it consists of seven speeches in praise of *Eros*. Plato uses the word *Eros* to designate love in all its varieties—at the bodily level as well as the soul- and spiritual levels. In these seven speeches the fascinating development of the forces of love is expressed in the most subtle way. Socrates is given the sixth speech, whereas the seventh, the climax of the work, is reserved for Alcibiades. The reader might think that Socrates ought to have the final word, but he has the penultimate speech and, in summary, says the following: All those who have spoken before me have given a eulogy of love without asking themselves whether what they were saying is really the truth. But I, Socrates, would like to say nothing but the simple, unembellished truth about love.

Thus the content of Socrates' speech is not a eulogy of love but purely and solely the truth about it. We can ask: Is it possible for there to be any more of a climax after Socrates' speech? Is it really possible to add anything to what the sage Socrates has articulated about the true mystery of love? It is. Plato knows a greater climax for the seventh speech.

As Socrates is finishing his speech, Alcibiades, one of Socrates' pupils, appears at the door in a drunken state. He doesn't give a speech about love but speaks about his teacher Socrates, and about how he, Alcibiades, feels loved by him. His speech is about how Socrates loves. Precisely because love is no less in development than humanity itself, we must imagine love between men in ancient Greece as something very specific, because people's inner experiences were different from what they are now. At the centre of the relationship between young men and their teacher Socrates, was the newly awakening ability to think independently, which at that time initially showed itself predominantly in men. This is evident in everything Alcibiades says about Socrates. This gives us once again a wonderful opportunity to convince ourselves of the changes that have taken place in the forces of love and thought over time, since today it goes without saying that women can think just as independently as men. And even the nature of the 'love' between men at that time would no longer be possible. We could perhaps add that with Greek philosophy one-sided masculine rationality began to pervade civilization, which in our time is waiting so urgently to be complemented by a logic of the heart.

Thus Socrates' speech, the sixth speech in Plato's *Symposium*, deals with the *truth* of love, and the seventh speech, in which Alcibiades bears witness to Socrates' love, deals with the *reality* of love. What Plato is perhaps wanting to say here is that it is one thing to *know* the truth about love theoretically, but quite another to actually *live* it, to realize love in one's life. Because Socrates lives love, because he can speak out of his own experience, he is the one in the best position to articulate the truth of love. And indeed, in his speech he goes through all love's stages of development. And when it comes to the most profound truth about love, he refers to the inspirations he has received from the divine Diotima. This name means roughly 'the one who reveres the Godhead'. This points to a spiritual being who draws from the wellspring of divine love the thoughts she communicates to Socrates.

Diotima, so Socrates says, had entrusted him with the following concerning love: the nature of love is such that it is ignited first of all by what we can see and touch—by a person's body, for example. It lies in the developmental dynamic of love that its starting-point is in bodily nature. Human beings fall in love initially with something they can see and touch; but they quickly realize that what is worthy of love is not the substance of a body but the immaterial form that makes the body beautiful. Every visible form is transient: here today, gone tomorrow. Every perceivable form, however, can be separated from the body and live on as an imperishable mental image in the soul, and this makes the soul more worthy of love than the body. In the creations of its imagination, the soul can preserve a rich treasure of beautiful forms.

Humanity is in love with the beauty of visible things, Diotima says, but beauty itself is not something material or physically perceptible. It is no less of a riddle or a mystery than love. It both reveals and conceals itself in everything we see, it appears everywhere, but only apparently so, it is the beautiful semblance in all things, but only semblance. A good example of this is the character of a person's gestures. The visible element, the body itself, is not what is important but rather the form it takes on. But this in turn is only made visible through the body. And it is precisely this hide-and-seek that makes the beautiful so irresistible. Human beings love the things of the world because they feel that they make beauty visible and invisible. They make it evident that the best thing in life for our longing and love is invisible and remains so. The human soul loves the world because it makes visible the invisibility of beauty.

Human beings, according to Diotima's teaching to her pupil Socrates, fall in love with the inner tension that is created in them by this apparent appearance, this unconcealed concealment, this open secret of beauty. The world of appearance becomes all the more dear to them the more they are able to see in semblance the hidden existence of the beautiful, the eternal in everything transitory. Beauty appears at times more in one body, at times more in another, more or less imperfectly. Thus it comes about that, in their love for the beautiful, human beings gradually immerse themselves in the perfect, eternal and spiritual beauty of things in order to participate with their mind in the invisible sources that constantly bring forth the beautiful and the good. These shaping forces, which Plato calls 'ideas', are not 'some thing' but 'some one', they are none other than the 'Mothers' in Goethe's *Faust*. They are the beings who from time immemorial have created and maintained the world. They transform chaos, ugliness, that which is still 'chaotically' unordered, into our beautiful world, into the wonderful order that is our cosmos. The word *kosmein* (from which our word *cosmetics* is derived) means 'to order', 'to make beautiful', 'to adorn'. For the Greeks, creation was a glorious beautification, every act of creation was an ordering, an adorning. They thought that only the artistic imagination of divine beings could bring forth such a beautiful *kosmos* in which people live. And man was created in the image of the Godhead because the human being too is an imaginative artist. He can comprehend and wonder at the beautiful and the good in creation because he bears in himself the same divine spirit that has formed the world so wonderfully. Only a soul that is already drawn towards the beautiful can love the beauty of creation; only a mind that is created by and for the good can recognize the morally good in creation. The world is the imagination-become-visible of creative artists, created for the love of humanity so as to make possible for every human being the joyful experience of the imagination of love.


## First love and hate

The harmless nature of a love given to us by nature is most beautifully expressed in the love that each person has for themselves. An erroneous morality has caused much harm by condemning this natural self-love, this egoism, as categorically bad. Self-love, since it is a gift of nature, can in itself be neither good nor bad. Only something performed in freedom can be morally good or bad. Our innate self-love is not free; the freedom lies only in how we deal with it. Self-love is quite simply indispensable. We could not live without this 'first love'; neither could we love anyone else without it. Our love of self is what gives us the possibility of being 'someone' in the first place. If I were a 'no one', if I were nothing, if I had created nothing in myself and for myself, I would have nothing to give others.

Self-love becomes something positive when it is expanded into a love of the other; it only has negative consequences when it excludes love for others. A person can never love themself too much; things become questionable only if they love others too little. This 'second love', the love of others, cannot also be a gift of nature, for then it would be just as unfree as self-love. But because each individual can decide anew every day to give their love to others, it is possible for a person to change even their self-love into a love that is free.

Anyone who thinks they don't love themself is merely deluded. Even a suicide acts out of self-love. Someone who takes their own life is promising themself some advantage from it, otherwise they couldn't kill themself. The only 'compelling' reason capable of inducing a suicide to take their own life is the conviction that by their deed they will improve their situation. 'I'd rather die,' they say. They are convinced it would be better for them to cease living.

If we have first to become something, to be something, before we can love others, then hate is precisely the power that shows up like a force of nature when we fear we are being overrun by others. We defend ourselves with the power of 'hate' against anything that threatens our being or impairs our development. Seen in this light, hate is a radical form of self-love, is loyalty to oneself, the defence of one's autonomy.

A person who was incapable of defending themself against threatening encroachments from others, who let themself succumb completely to the demands of others, or who even allowed themself to become the blind executor of others' orders, in the end would extinguish themself and would not be capable of loving others. What we call 'hate', in its natural form, is neither good nor bad but quite simply essential for development. It is the force by which we all defend ourselves against any kind of external dominance—and *have* to defend ourselves! Wherever there is an intention from outside to force us against the wall, whenever someone tries to make us into an instrument of their own purposes, the natural response is to evoke hatred, which is none other than the primal force in the human being of self-defence and autonomy.

Self-assertion is just as important as devotion to others. Only when I repel everything that threatens my being, when I am in a position to defend myself against everything that jeopardizes my independence, can I also find the power in myself to do something, out of myself and in full freedom, for others. On a path of inner development, human beings learn to love other people, beings, and things, and the longing grows in them to be able to encompass all people, all the beings of nature, in their love.

If we were all only concerned with our own affairs, hardly anyone would experience the real beauty and goodness that life can offer. A person who only loves themselves is left alone by others, they have to go without the love that only others can bring them. A pure egotist is some-one who has the least love for themselves. The person who is focused on others, is interested in them and supports them, will be able to savour life in all its richness. They will engender the wish in others to repay love with love. Someone who loves more and more people is also loved by more and more people. But if they do so in order to be loved, then they are not loving the others but only themself. Accordingly they will experience less love in return.


## Developmental stages of 'hate'

In order for the human principle in us to come to the fore in increasingly pure form, love must be able to repulse everything that is contra-hu-man. It has to 'hate', has to oppose, everything that can diminish human worth. And what is it that takes away some of our humanity, what is it that makes us morally of less value? What are the forms of inhumanity that evoke a healthy 'hate'?

Firstly there are all the forms of *untruth* and *lying* for which every thinking person has a profound aversion. We feel them to be humanly unworthy because they undermine our search for truth; they evoke an automatic kind of hatred in us because deception and deceit mislead us, they hold us back from the truth. We must abhor everything that hin-ders us in our knowledge of truth, to which we aspire in our innermost being because in the last analysis only this can make us happy.

If I fail to cultivate my innate aspiration for truth, I become spiri-tually impoverished. The more inadequate my thinking and the less

I understand of the human being and the world, the more helplessly I am at the mercy of all kinds of deceptive manoeuvrings. And the majority of people who feel lied to and deceived in this way respond to this experience with one of the many forms of hate.

The second thing that provokes feelings of hatred is *egotism in others*, because under its effect we feel short-changed. Short-sighted self-love leads people to exploit each other. Thus we all spontaneously direct hatred towards any attempt by others to use us for their own purposes. Only gradually do people realize that the situation for all can only improve when everyone tries no longer to direct their hatred towards the egotism of others, but against their own. This inner change is the beginning of love for others.

The third kind of hate is directly concerned with the physical and corporeal sphere. It consists in the fact that every person must resist with all the power of their being anything that impairs the health of the body: in short, all forms of *sickness*. We oppose anything that threatens our body, since this is the foundation of our whole existence. The deeply felt abhorrence of any kind of torture is a recognition of the preciousness, and indeed the inviolability, of the physical body. Dissipation and asceticism are equally contrary to this healthy feeling since they both compromise the health of the body.

Given to us by nature, this threefold hatred of untruth, egotism, and sickness is the prerequisite for the free development of threefold love in human beings: love of the body, of the soul, and of the spirit. In loving the truth we love the spirit in ourselves and in every other person. When we love others we also love the beauty of our own soul and the soul of the other. And our striving for bodily health expresses our love for the earthly forces that keep each one of us alive.

The more inwardly free human beings become, the more they are liberated from their hatred. This is simply because they need it less and less. They begin to realize that what they hate *outside* themselves is something worthy of hate that they carry *in themselves*, and what they are called upon to conquer. They begin to see that what they hate in another can only be what they themselves still have to overcome.

Every feeling of hatred that rises up in me can become a task for me in working on myself. When I hate someone's lies, what is it that I so abhor in reality? It is the fact that I am still prone to being lied to and deceived. It is difficult for me to admit that I'm being fooled, that people can deceive me so easily. Evidently this means nothing less than that at the moment I am not yet always able to distinguish truth from untruth. If I were able to do so, the other could lie to me as much as they wanted, I would notice it immediately and would not have to hate their lies, I wouldn't be angered by them because I could protect myself from them.

As long as I am unable to judge what comes to meet me from outside—perhaps because I lack experience—I just have to wait with my judgement. In this way I can avoid being fooled or led astray. I am healed of my hatred when I realize that my hatred towards the outer world is actually only pointing me to what I still have to overcome in myself. A person who was really perfect could not hate any thing or any one.

As with lies, I also hate the egotism of others if I feel exploited by them in any way. And what is *this* hatred telling me? It tells me: You want to overcome your own egotism which tempts you no less often to use others only as a means for your own personal purposes. You want to overcome what makes you hateful or ugly in their eyes, because you want to feel their love and not their hate.

No one has the right to expect others to treat them more lovingly than they treat others. My innate 'hatred', my aversion to the egotism of others, is healthy because it stimulates me to overcome my own egotism. If my egotism is what makes me 'worthy of hate', then the more I 'hate' the egotism in myself and overcome it, the more I make myself 'worthy of love'. Nature has put a great love for one's own freedom into the human heart—healthy self-love—and it is up to human beings, in the course of their life, to transform this innate love for freedom into an achieved freedom of love—which encompasses more and more people.

The deepest truths of life can only be expressed by apparent contradictions or paradoxes. One such contradiction would be that I can only allow myself to let others do what they want when they cannot harm me, even though they might hurt me! When, for example, someone tricks me out of ten thousand euros, does this harm me? There is a difference whether I say they have caused me to have ten thousand euros less (an objective statement of fact), or whether I think they have harmed me (a personal feeling). If I think they have harmed me, I am not stating an objective fact but am expressing my purely subjective experience of the event. I could also have the attitude of: 'So much the better! I don't feel wronged at all. On the contrary, now I have ten thousand fewer things to worry about.' A fine contradiction! Someone in the same situation might perhaps say, 'And I needed that money so urgently in my life!' We could reply, 'If you needed it for your life, how have you managed to live up to now without spending it?'

The power to love all people is the salt that gives life taste. The power to hate everything that hinders people from loving more and more, is the pepper that gives life spice.

## Love is more than a feeling

How can lovelessness, inner indifference, be overcome? If it is true that the most bitter enemy of love is its absence, its omission, then the more we are able to widen the circle of people dear to us, who we care for, and who we are prepared to support, the more beautiful life becomes.

Love is the power of the heart to find everything in the world interesting. There is nothing that is not worthy of our attention. Yet it is not the task of the world to interest people—if it were, people would be underemployed if not actually unemployed!—but rather it is the task of human beings themselves to be interested in the world. For someone who is interested in everything, everything is interesting, and this fact makes them the happiest person in the world.

The important question therefore is: How do we manage to be interested in increasingly more people? The cliff that must be circumnavigated here is the widespread view that love is only a feeling, a feeling that arises in us by itself, that simply appears without our having to do anything. If we look at it more closely, however, we have to admit that feelings are never anything more than a reverberation in the soul of the many diverse events we perceive in the external world. Love as a feeling is also the inner response to a music that must initially sound outside ourselves. As long as love is only felt, is only a feeling, it remains self-love. It broadens out to a love of others when this feeling is connected with thinking and will. If I try with my thinking to understand the other better and better, and then act out of this understanding in a way that is helpful to the other, then what was initially just a feeling in me or self-love becomes increasingly a true love. The feeling is pure self-enjoyment; self-love belongs to the beautiful gifts of nature. Only my thinking, my striving for objective understanding of the human being and the world, transforms my self-love into love for other people.

The warmth of love a person feels in themself is always the echo of the love they have directed to the beings around them. It is so important to them to enjoy this beneficent feeling of love that they often lose sight of the fact that the feeling can only be generated from love that has already been given. What is happiness if not a raying back to us of what we have given to others! Self-love by itself simply fills us with longing; love for others brings us joy. A person can only experience the joy of love in themself if they have really managed to turn their focus on others, to become involved in others, to know how to act wherever others are in need. Self-love becomes increasingly a love of humankind when we learn to love ourselves for the sake of another, and to love others for the sake of ourselves. In no other way do the parts of an organism relate to each other, and this is the law according to which all life develops.

We can often have the impression that there is more happiness in being loved than in loving. It might also appear that we can enjoy being loved without ourselves loving. Certainly I can be happy if someone tells me they love me, just as I can enjoy it when I look at the starry heavens or the gloriously blue sea. On the other hand, someone I don't love would find it hard to love me—unless they were already very far advanced in their development. And if it were the starry heavens in themselves that moved me so deeply, then they would have to move everyone in the same way, just as everyone who jumps into water gets wet. But that isn't how it is: the world can only move those who are inwardly mobile, who activate the power of interest in themselves. One who approaches the thousand wonders of the world with their own wonder, one who is able to wonder at the mysteries of life, is moved ever more deeply by the world. If I am incapable of any kind of inner response, the beauty of the world leaves me cold, it can even really get on my nerves when others are full of wonder at it, in the same way that 'love' extended towards me can just be a nuisance.

Love works like healthy circulation: the attention that someone gives to others, fills that person's heart with joy; this joy in turn strengthens their resolve to love all the world. Anyone at any moment in their life can ask: What is it in my surroundings that should have priority for my attention right now? And when they see how much and in how many directions things are waiting for them to open their heart, they will be convinced that it is always possible for them to bestow love, that the human heart has always known the paths of love.

# 2. Love and Sexuality

*Squaring the Circle*

## The past and future of the masculine and the feminine

We find a very particular experience of love in the mutual attraction of the sexes. Not without justification is it said that the story of man and woman is as old as the world. The Latin word for sex, *sexus*, comes from *secare*, meaning to cut, to separate (the German word *sägen* = to saw, comes from the same root). In the fourth of the seven speeches on the theme of love in Plato's *Symposium*, Aristophanes relates how Zeus split the originally bisexual human beings into two parts, for fear that they could become too strong and challenge his power. *Divide et impera*, 'divide and rule', was the later motto of the Romans who made this the principle for their dominance. The Greek myth tells us that the original human being, before being divided by Zeus into two parts, was man and woman in one. These bisexual human beings, according to the *Symposium*, had started to have great aspirations and threatened to gain access to Olympus and attack the gods. By separating them into two sexes, Zeus weakened them. They could no longer commit 'outrages', especially since from now on each part was fully occupied with looking for its lost half in order to reunite with it!

This beautiful myth expressing a basic truth about the evolution of humanity and love, is the Greek version of something also found in the Bible. It says there: 'And God created man, in the likeness of God created he him; male and female created he them.' If God created man in His own image, this can only mean that He created him as a perfect complete being. For God is perfection, and if He creates man in His own image, He can only create him as a totality—male *and* female in one, not as man *or* woman. A more faithful translation of the Hebrew text would be: 'God created the human being as man and woman in one.' The image of the later separation of Eve from Adam's rib depicts in a beautiful way that the human being only later became either male or female. From the original wholeness of Adam there came two types of human being, different and separated from each other, who have been looking for each other ever since. Thus the original Adam of the Bible can in no way be referring to a man but to the original male-female human being.

Since the separation of the sexes, the unfolding of the long love story between woman and man has virtually epitomized the evolution of humanity itself. Understanding evolution also involves understanding how the relationship between man and woman has changed over the course of time. In this long history we can distinguish three chief phases:

- In the beginning there was unity: the hermaphroditic, androgynous Adam (from Greek *aner, andros* = man; and *gyne* = woman), who was man and woman in one.
- The second stage, where we find ourselves today, arises by the separating of the sexes, the separation of humanity into male and female halves, into men and women.
- The third stage, the goal of evolution, is the gradual reunification of the masculine and feminine in each person. Evolution aspires to the uniting at a higher level of the two halves that are seeking each other; higher in the sense that it is achieved by people in freedom.

The meaning of the separation of the sexes is that each half is thereby given the task of gaining the other half through free striving. One can't strive after something one already has as a gift of nature; one can't become more of what one already is. And what makes us happier: being something or becoming something? As surprising as it may sound, striving after something beautiful gives us far more joy than anything we have already achieved. We need only think of a human life: every young person wants to *become* old, but no one want to *be* old. This is why 'senior citizens' are politely called 'elderly' and not 'old', because 'elderly' sounds younger than 'old'. All this is just to say that *becoming*, striving, is the greatest happiness a human being can have. And to strive after something means nothing less than to *love* it. The love between a man and a woman is a ceaseless striving towards one another, a searching for each other, a yearning and longing for each other. The meaning of the separation of the sexes is their mutual love, their striving to be reunited.

If we ask why striving for something gives us more joy than anything we already possess, the answer can only be that in striving, in seeking, human beings experience their highest degree of freedom, their creative imagination, the free development of their best forces, above all the power of love. Whether and how we strive, what we strive for, depends entirely on our ingenuity. There is far less initiative possible in what we already have, in what we have already become. Only in striving towards something new do we feel completely free. Here we approach from another side the fact that to love and to be free are fundamentally one and the same thing. Together they make the human being happy.

## Man and Woman: related and foreign

Everything that is material is external and foreign to us. When it comes to the physical and material world, we can only make our own what we can transform into our thoughts and mental images. A quartz crystal only becomes a component of my inner life when, via my perception, I form a mental picture or concept of it. I can never penetrate directly into its substance; that remains completely external to what I experience inside myself, it remains completely foreign.

Applying this to our treatment of sexuality, this means that I can never share with anyone else the sensations or stimuli that are dependent on my body, I can only experience them entirely alone. Likewise I cannot share the sensations that are aroused in the body of another since the physical matter of their body is external to me and therefore foreign. Every person is alone in their body. And because male and female bodies are biologically fundamentally different, they generate stimuli and inner experiences that can be experienced only by a man or a woman. Typically speaking, no man can experience female bodily sensations, and no woman can feel sensations that can be stimulated only in a male body. Every person has their own sensations of warmth, cold, smell, taste, and pain, everyone feels their own hunger, thirst, or itch. No one can transpose their 'goosebumps' to someone else; only yawning, perhaps, but that is only because the emotional boredom is likewise transferred. The whole meaning of the body is that it gives each of us the possibility of closing off in ourselves and thus achieving a certain independence.

Apart from bodily sensations, everyone also experiences *feelings* that are not fully dependent on the state of the body but can be of a purely emotional or soul nature. No one would hold their body responsible for the anger they feel at an insult, the pleasure at a visit from a friend, in the same way they would for a headache, hunger, or their short-sightedness. When feelings are not aroused by bodily sensations, it is easier to convey them to other people. Naturally this is not to say that one person's feelings are the same as another's, but it is easier to share purely emotional things with someone else than what we are experiencing in our body. For example, when I share the happiness of a friend who has passed an exam with a high mark, it is not their happiness that I experience directly, but rather the fact that I can empathize and participate in their happiness. Thus it is only at the soul level that a real union between a man and a woman is possible, which is due to this faculty of empathy, of shared experience and shared feeling.

Apart from sensations determined by the body, and soul-born feelings, people also have *thoughts* created in the mind. In the experience of thinking, the opposition, the polarity of male and female, is completely dissolved; here there are no more boundaries to union. In the world of thought, in the world of spirit, man and woman can really become one; in the feeling-world of the soul the human being swings to and fro between union and isolation; in the bodily realm, each is on their own, enclosed in their own world. Thus through spirit, soul, and body the human being can experience love in different forms: as communion of the mind, as conversation between soul and soul, and as self-feeling through the body.


## What makes people free is good

The biological laws of sexuality apply to both humans and animals. Nevertheless, human beings cannot express their sexuality in the same way as animals because, unlike the animal soul, the human soul is characterized by the 'I', by the individual spirit, which animals do not have. Seen in this light, human beings are most 'animal' in their body, and most 'human' in their mind or spirit. The soul again oscillates between the natural and the spiritual worlds, which are experienced as opposites. It connects and enriches both worlds, and is itself enriched by both.

Animals are not free in their behaviour regarding their body, they have to follow their nature-given instincts. Although human beings have animal-like drives, they also have, in contrast to the animal, the faculty of thinking about these drives and their meaning. How would it be if, in a moment of self-reflection, a lion were able to say: 'I was not free in my habit of eating people. I will bear witness to my freedom by loving all people and animals from now on, instead of eating them.' Such human 'pricks of conscience' are unknown to animals. People, on the other hand, are not forced to the same extent by their natural impulses because they can make them the tool for their freely chosen goals. Once the sex drive is awakened in the animal, it has to follow it. Human beings have freedom in how they act with regard to this drive.

And because procreation itself follows natural laws in which human freedom plays no part, human beings are only free to decide *whether* they are going to enter this play of forces in nature or not. We are considerably more circumspect and freer when first deciding to engage with the forces of sexuality than we are once submerged in their power and feel positively overwhelmed by the forces of nature.

As far as the working of nature in the human being goes, it is not a question of morality, of good and bad, and most certainly not of love and freedom. Only when we can choose between different behaviours do we have the possibility of acting in a way that is morally good or bad. Only then does human freedom come into consideration at all, and consequently the responsibility of the individual for their actions.

How would someone who valued their freedom wish to deal with sexuality? Since people are very different, there can be nothing that is good or bad in the same way for everyone. Many things that can advance the personal development of one person can be a hindrance to another. The question, for example, whether it would be right for me to have a child or not, clearly shows that there is no answer here that applies to everyone, and purely theoretical considerations will not get us very far. I find the right answer for me alone in my heart, and in the confidence that I will cope with my life whatever my decision.

In relation to sexuality we can also say: If my inner freedom is important to me, then everything that makes me freer must be good for me, and everything that compels me to give up my freedom, even only partially, is not good. Only to the extent that freedom and unfreedom have characteristics that are universally valid can we speak about sexuality in general and ask ourselves which way of dealing with these forces makes people—all people—freer, and which not.

# Sexuality on the path to freedom

There was considerable movement in the course of the twentieth century in how sexuality is dealt with. For a long time 'sex' and 'freedom' were considered synonymous, 'sexual liberation' was simply 'in'. People wanted to finally clear away all the irksome rules and prohibitions of a repressive morality. What was perhaps often overlooked is the fact that sexuality, a concept applicable to the physical realm, and freedom, a quality of the mind, are in a certain sense opposites. Our natural drives can easily give us the impression that we are free with respect to them because the decision to give ourselves up to their power is often an entirely free one. This does not mean, however, that we remain equally free after we have engaged with them. The decision to drink a bottle of vodka or whisky may well be a free one, but this does not mean that the person, once drunk, is still free. An aspect of freedom is the fact that we can freely decide to give it up, as when someone decides to take their own life.

The condition of the body that best enables the experience of freedom is *health*. And the body is most healthy when we don't notice it at all. A violin serves its purpose best when it is so well tuned, and the musician plays so superbly, that we become fully absorbed in the music. But as soon as something goes wrong with the instrument, all our attention is immediately drawn to that fact and the wonderful musical experience is over. It is the same with us: we only notice the instrument of our body when something is wrong and we no longer feel free to concentrate fully on our activities and surroundings.

A characteristic of modern materialism is its fixation on the body. And because of the preoccupation with this as an 'object'—from wellness holidays to fitness studios to sport—many people do not realize that the body cannot be an end in itself, but is designed as an instrument for the melodies of the soul and for the creations of the mind, for the experiences of mutual affection among people, and for the discoveries of thought. Such notions are far from wanting to spoil any pleasures of the body such as eating or enjoying nature. Quite the reverse: someone who eats in order to be as healthy as possible and thus to savour life to the full at all levels, will be able to enjoy their food more than someone who, instead of eating in order to live an ever better life, lives to eat with ever more relish. One who knows no greater happiness than enjoying food—no matter how sophisticated and delicious the food may be—is literally impoverished because they have no idea what they are missing, what other far more 'delicious fare' life has to offer.

The purpose of life is to give us the possibility of discovering what kind of happiness can be experienced in soul and spirit through love and freedom. Pleasures dependent on the body, since these are given as a gift from nature, cannot make us happier than pleasures of the mind which can only be attained in freedom. We need only look at what is written in the biography of a person over the years. When we are very small, our greatest pleasure is to drink milk and be rocked. When we are a bit bigger, what we like most is perhaps a bar of chocolate or a pizza, and there is nothing better than having our own toy or a bicycle. When we are a bit older, our greatest happiness is in girls or boys, and a few years later we perhaps like particularly to go to the cinema or a night-club, or we develop a passion for the theatre or music, whereby we are already in the realm of pleasures of the soul that are more determined by our preferences than by the body.

When a few more years have gone by, and a strong interest has awakened in mathematics, or medicine, agriculture, travel, finance, history, trade, anthropology, ship-building, cuisine, science, philosophy, the art of living and so on, we are dealing with the pleasure of knowledge which is of a more mental or spiritual nature. In this realm, the most beautiful pleasures do not come by themselves: each individual has to do something to attain them! Perhaps we have to practise a great deal, have to work hard on ourselves, in order to discover or create something. At all events the free decision to engage in questions of knowledge is based on our personal inclination and requires our initiative in some form or another. But when we choose our own tasks, when we determine our own direction, our activity will give us great satisfaction.

All the pleasures we can experience through the body are given us by nature. What fulfils us mentally has to be freely worked for. But only in this way will we make our soul truly happy. As a young person we have a great right to be 'natural', and in old age we have the greater right to be ever more free. The farther we advance along the path of freedom, the more beautiful and meaningful life becomes. It is indeed for this reason that we, and particularly women, are procreative in a different way in the first half of life than in the second. We have youth for procreation (*Zeugung*), and old age for conviction (*Überzeugung*), for procreation through free mental-spiritual creativity. It is not by chance that the body in youth is beautiful and strong, whereas in later years spiritual depth and wisdom can come to the fore.

Much-praised eroticism is seen as art, as free play with the forces of nature, especially with the sex drive. Many ask whether this art couldn't be exercised with more imagination, whether it could become an experience of genuine freedom, if not even of a deeper liberation from all compulsion? Many have long since ceased to see eroticism exclusively as what plays out in the body, but as applying also—and in general this applies more to women than to men—to what is experienced in the heart, in the world of feelings. In every act of love, many see something morally lofty, a loving devotion to one's partner. There are also people who seek a religious experience in sexuality, and there are many 'sacred scriptures' of the East to which they feel able to refer. We need only recall certain interpretations of the Kama Sutra or the thousands-year-old tradition of Tantra.

And yet when we look at it more closely we have to say that people are no less impoverished by a glorification of sexuality than by its demonization. The cult of the body and the body's mortification both have in common the need to 'check off' the theme of human and natural forces once and for all. We want to see the matter finally settled by either idealizing everything of an instinctive nature or by deprecating it. If we are permanently wedded to the notion that human instincts simply *are* either good or bad, we spare ourselves the essential daily struggle of letting them *become* something good over and over again. What is good for the human being however, as we observed previously, is constant development, and thus also the striving for a proper balance between body and mind, nature and freedom. Both the cult of the body and hatred of the body bring all inner development to a standstill. We make things easy for ourselves when we put a moral label on instinctive forces and assert that they are of one nature or another. But we can only develop when we seek daily for the proper harmony of all our forces.


## 'Enjoying' the physical and the spiritual at the same time?

One who looks for happiness purely in sexuality may sooner or later have the same experience as one who tries to square the circle: namely, that it can't be done. If one stresses the sexual element in love, one is looking for fulfilment where there isn't any. If I expect the forces of nature to give me the joyful experience of freedom, I will experience one disappointment after another. We experience happiness when we use all our natural forces to bring forth in freedom something that is more than nature. Nature makes happiness possible for each person, but cannot bestow it itself. It has to leave that experience to our development towards inner freedom.

Here we can look for greater clarity and ask the question: Why should it not be possible to savour fully and entirely both bodily and spiritual pleasures? What is to prevent human beings from enjoying, to the fullest degree and at the same time, both the sensations of the body and the discoveries of the mind? Would this not be the epitome of the greatest possible happiness? To find an answer to this question it would perhaps be helpful, if not an actual requirement, to refrain from any preconceived justification or condemnation. This will make it possible to observe as objectively as possible what is going on in every woman and man in the moments when the forces of the sex drive gain the upper hand, when sensations determined by the body are stronger than feelings or thoughts.

The *first observation* is that the more I give myself over to the forces of nature in my body, the less free I feel to decide for myself what I am doing. I feel increasingly dulled in my consciousness, my willpower decreases to the same extent that I have the feeling of 'letting myself go'. If the voice of conscience begins to speak here, I will perhaps try to silence it by telling myself that it is simply beautiful, even something worth striving for, to give oneself up to the wisdom of nature. People should stop always trying to control nature. Why not give her free rein, why not trust her?

Looked at more closely, it is precisely this need for justification that makes it possible to see that devotion to the body precludes us from simultaneous activity in our innermost core. We can't be inwardly passive and active at the same time. Life presents each of us with this choice: to decide either for the one or the other. Inner freedom, initiative of the will, is only possible by overcoming our instinctive nature, the nature in us that is unfree. Human beings are never free; they can only become free over and over again by repeatedly liberating themselves from all the necessary conditions of nature. These, however, have to be there, because only in confronting them can we overcome and free ourselves from them.

Becoming free for human beings means, in every moment and every situation in life, being 'stronger' than the nature in them. Being free means having a strong will. Each time I succumb to an urge, I weaken my will and make myself a little bit less free. But each time I manage to master my nature, I strengthen my will forces, and my inner freedom grows. I cannot be both master and servant in my own house. My body is always either my servant or my master; it can't be both at once. But the more I allow it to be my master, the more it will push me out of this role. This can go so far that bodily needs gain the upper hand to the extent that a person begins to feel themselves in a state of addiction. This condition can definitely be compared to the condition otherwise seen in addicts.

A *second observation* tells us that our instinctive forces are not individual, since drives, which we have in common with animals, are not an expression of our uniqueness. They belong to our nature and we share them with all other human beings, with the entire human race. When I give myself up to these natural forces, I must at the same time renounce expressing myself as a unique individuality. I cannot live out an instinct that works the same way in all people and at the same time express myself in a completely individual way. Everything that is spiritual or of a soul nature—such as the pursuit of knowledge or devotion to a friend—allows a maximum of individualization, because it can be expressed in countless ways and in infinite shades. By contrast, instinct allows very little scope for the personal and individual. Put in musical terms, the creations of the mind give the soul innumerable themes and limitless possibilities for individual variation. But when the soul gives itself over to the body, it is always the same pieces that play out in few original variations.

Some see eroticism as the art of increasing self-pleasure through the body to its furthest possible limits. For them the basic rule of the game is the same as in the free market economy: if everyone looks after themself, then everyone is looked after. But this is not how it is in reality. A mere summation of egotisms can never result in love for the other. On the contrary, if a man or woman are both seeking only to maximize their own pleasure through the body of the other, the inner experience in the soul is that of a twofold isolation, a double loneliness, because each is using the other only to strengthen their own self-centredness.

We can compare eroticism with the art of cookery: the preparation of dishes can be refined more and more to increase dining pleasure in a thousand ways. But we have to ask: Can the enjoyment of the body as such, in whatever form, make us happy, or can we really only become happy by experiencing our body as a tool for the 'pleasures' of the soul and spirit? If the latter is the case, fixation on the body cannot make us happy—not, however, because it is morally sinful according to a morality imposed from without, but the reverse: because it is a pity, indeed a real sin, to settle for the sake of ease for a half happiness instead of striving for full happiness.

The human soul is so constituted that it would like always to make everything of a bodily nature an instrument for the experiences of the spirit. This lies in its nature. It is the princess we all know from fairy tales. She waits longingly for the prince who will release her from her enchantment. Banishment into the forces of nature extinguishes the unique aspect that every soul seeks in its own spirit. When the soul is able to unfold its imagination freely, when an individual with all their strength is able to love and live out the completely individual ideals of their spirit, they then experience their greatest happiness.

This can lead us to a *third observation*: when I experience primarily the forces of my body, I shut myself off in my own world of experience, which isolates me from other people. In our time, the body is so much in the foreground that what many people know is almost exclusively only body-related experiences. They don't even know what we are talking about when we speak of soul or spirit. But it is precisely the pervasive cult of the body that increasingly isolates people from each other, because one person can experience nothing of what another feels internally, triggered by the processes of their body. The task of the body, as already indicated, lies precisely in the fact that it enables us to experience ourselves as a being separate from others. This experience is essential for the experience of freedom. Only we should not look for an expression of love—devotion to another—where we are most closed off in ourselves.

A *fourth observation* can show us that the human spirit is correspondingly dulled to the extent that we surrender to the experience of a drive. However, it is important to clarify what we mean here by a 'drive'. Without even having thought about it, everyone knows from their own experience the difference between 'being driven' and 'driving oneself'.

In the first case we feel more or less powerless, in the second case, more or less free.

When I hit a steep, slippery track and find I can no longer stop or control my ride, I feel 'driven' by forces I have little influence over. On the other hand, if I run on a flat track, I can adjust or stop my movement at any time. In this case I feel free because the impulse for the movement comes from myself; it is consciously willed by me. Here I am not driven, but drive myself. It is precisely in this sense that the difference between drives and freedom is meant here. This shows clearly that a free inner activity like thinking is experienced quite differently from the action of an instinct that operates in me in a way that does not lie in my freedom.

The 'orgasms' of the body and of the mind or spirit are mutually exclusive, like unfreedom and freedom. The procreative processes of the body and of the mind cannot be experienced at the same time. Just as we extinguish love, the innate force of the soul, when we close ourselves entirely in our experience of the body, so too, by merging with the sensations of the body, we dull our thinking, the primal power of the spirit.

Rapture of the senses and a clear head cannot be experienced simultaneously. When I have strong feelings of pleasure or pain, I am not able to use my body at the same time as a willed instrument for the brightest flashes of thought. Forces of life and consciousness stand in opposition to one another, and are mutually dependent. Unfolding consciousness always means using up life-forces and killing them. We can only build up new life-forces by withdrawing or shutting down our consciousness, as happens when we sleep.

It is simply in the nature of sexual arousal, no matter what the details of how it is experienced, that it runs counter to calmly considered thinking. One has to 'let go' of one's consciousness so that nature can operate unhindered. And if a person tries during the sexual act to think of the other, they put their own purely physical needs aside and in this way find an emotional satisfaction which is of a completely different kind from the purely bodily one.

There is much public discussion today of homosexuality. For many people, putting homosexual marriage on an equal footing with traditional marriage is an important achievement of a free society. Every kind of relationship between two people—as long as it does not involve an under-age child whose rights must be legally protected—is a matter solely for the individuals concerned, irrespective of whether they are of the same or different genders. When a relationship between two people of the same sex is not only one of friendship or emotional affection but also involves the sex drive so that bodily experience comes to the fore, the observations mentioned above are equally applicable.

## From the suffering of Amfortas to the compassion of Parzival

In the spirit of Christianity, love is paramount, since it is said that human beings cannot approach the Godhead in wisdom nor through power, but only in love. Human beings can only experience the all-wise, all-powerful God as being infinitely superior, infinitely far. But there is no 'all-love' of God, because God has poured a drop of His own love into every human heart. Human beings have the possibility to permeate each of their actions with the warmth of divine love.

The Christian Gospels speak of the mystery of love in living pictures, for example where Christ meets the woman taken in adultery. One day the scribes and the Pharisees bring a woman to him and say: 'Rabbi, this woman was caught in the very act of adultery. The law of Moses says she must be stoned. What do you say?' These men must have thought: He won't be able to talk himself out of this, because if he says we should not stone her, he is going against the law of Moses, and if he says we should stone her, he will contradict himself and all his previous babblings about love and forgiveness. But Jesus surprises them with his answer: 'Let him who is without sin cast the first stone.'

The Gospel says that when they heard this, they all went away, one after the other, beginning with the oldest. Why the oldest first? Because the older we get, the more we have on our slate. In the end Christ is alone with the woman and says, 'Has no one condemned you? I also do not condemn you.' There is no point in condemning people. What helps is to love them and encourage them to keep moving forward. What Christ wishes to tell the woman is: You can always learn from your deeds, particularly from your mistakes. Just keep going, live, never stop in your development! Usually this part is translated as: 'Go and sin no more.' This 'go' really says nothing. The Greek *poreuo* does not just mean a physical going, it means in general 'to be on one's way', 'to move forwards', also in the sense of 'to add to your learning', 'to inwardly develop further'.

Christ wants to say to the woman that she should continually strive in order to undo the 'sin'. He has come to help every individual overcome bit by bit the aspect of instinct that makes us unfree. We experience freedom and happiness in what we overcome on a daily basis, not in what we have already overcome. And in order to be able to experience this daily liberation from our drives, the drives have to be there, they must exercise their power. Thus Christ points to a path we can walk in our dealings with our sex drive. He neither condemns adultery nor does he condone it. He draws attention to the human being's inner development and leaves it to the freedom of the individual—in this case the adulteress—whether they choose to take this path or not.

Another wonderful image can be found in *Parzival*. This work is, in the versions by both Wolfram von Eschenbach and Chrétien de Troyes, among the most beautiful and profound things to be produced by the Christian Middle Ages. It depicts a decisive moment in Parzival's inner path when he is led for the first time to the Grail Castle and brought before the gravely wounded and languishing King Amfortas, the guardian of the Grail. Parzival fails to ask him about his suffering. He fails to do so because the forces of compassion and love in him are not yet sufficiently developed.

Parzival must learn that to love means to take another into one's heart, to empathize with their pain, to make their inner struggle one's own, to want to help them. On his first visit, when faced with the suffering of the other, he is silent, he is not yet able to feel compassion. He will first have to experience the pain of Amfortas' wound 'in his own body', in his own soul, before he can feel 'com-passion'. Only one's own suffering opens the heart to the suffering of others also; only in this way can the power of compassion arise out of suffering. Parzival has only reached this stage of his development when he is permitted to enter the Grail Castle for the second time. Only now can he feel the suffering of the other so deeply that he asks the all-decisive question of King Amfortas, the question as to what causes him to ail so terribly. He receives the answer that it is a matter of a mysterious wound in the groin that never ceases to cause pain and never heals, and no one can explain why this is so or how the wound might be healed.

On his first visit to the Grail, Parzival was perhaps still too young. In youth, we are carried by the forces of nature in order gradually to learn what nature can give us and what she leaves to our freedom. Only a person who, for long enough and with all their energy, has sought the highest happiness in the joys of the senses without finding it, will be able to seek for something else, now out of freedom, out of the long-ing of love. Those who forbid themselves the joys of the sensual world without having experienced them sufficiently, suppress the driving forces of nature in themselves without transforming them, without having awakened spiritual drives, and thereby only make the natural forces stronger. They look for a 'higher love' not out of love but out of loveless duty, and not out of freedom but through submission to a law. All fear of nature, all contempt for her powers, brings the greatest harm to the forces of love in human beings, because nature is their mother who loves them above all else. The world of matter is crystallized love for the human spirit, made visible. In turning away from the physical world, of which our body is a part, we do not find the spirit but only the human being devoid of spirit and love. Only in an understanding love for the world of matter will we find the embodied spirit, the wounded Amfortas, who can only be released from his suffering by the forces of love and compassion.

And what will the person do who believes they have found happi-ness in the enjoyment of the senses because they experience no lack of *joie de vivre* there or lack of freedom? Such a person, for whom the gifts of nature are enough, will be the least likely to want to deaden these in themself as a means to compelling themself to search for the spirit, because compulsion can bring them neither spirit nor freedom. The goodness of destiny can reasonably do nothing but allow the fortu-nate 'natural man' all the time he needs on the way to the second Grail visit. No one can prescribe to another in what way or how quickly their inner development should proceed. And a person would be living in serious delusion if they imagined themself already on the second visit to the Grail Castle without having first travelled the long road there step by step.

It is also in this sense that Goethe's *Faust* is to be understood. The highs and lows of the second part of this work can only be experienced by one who has fully lived and suffered the first part, the mysteries of sensual love. This is also the meaning of the parable in the Gospel where it is said that heaven rejoices more for one who has lost themself and found themself again, than for the one who has shunned the experience of first love, the abyss of freedom.

Our nature of drives and urges is the necessary fall in our evolution of love which had to become unfree so that a greater, freely achieved love, can be experienced through our liberation from drives. Through the equally necessary fall of consciousness, human beings became dependent on their physical brain, their thoughts became lifeless mirrored images of external reality. It is indeed the outermost surface of the world that we experience in this way. This makes us terribly superficial, for with this kind of thinking we can comprehend only the laws of what is dead and mechanical.

The Fall of love and consciousness is the twofold gift of divine love to human beings, who thereby receive the task of attaining their freedom themselves; for only in the daily overcoming of the consequences of the Fall can humanity become ever freer. But this also means that Amfortas' wound cannot, and may not, be healed by submission to moral commandments or merely by the expectation of being healed by divine grace, so to speak, 'instantaneously'. Only by a conscious and gradual inner transformation can human beings attain the freedom which heals the inherited wound. Only one who loves the spirit with all the power of their soul is able to overcome the inexorable nature of instinct without suppressing it.

In an artistic image, Amfortas' wound depicts how human consciousness, through its connection with the body, is cut off from experience of the spirit. Because matter and spirit diverge in human consciousness, humanity experiences a wound that has caused it pain for millennia. Due to human thinking submersing itself ever deeper into matter, the human I has split. The 'everyday' lower ego has devoted itself entirely to the earthly world and to self-love shut off in itself, thereby losing sight of the true, the higher Ego. People no longer know whether reality is what they can see and touch, or whether it is the spirit whose whereabouts they are no longer so sure of, or indeed whether it exists at all.

For a very long time the human being Amfortas has already suffered from being dominated by forces of nature whose innermost being expresses itself in the reproductive drive—for this is how the wound in the groin area is to be understood. Amfortas' wound is in the place where the Scorpion pushes its deadly sting into man, this 'sting of the flesh', which gave so much trouble to Saul of Tarsus, better known as Saint Paul. Paul, too, asked to be freed from the pain of this wound once and for all, and in answer had to hear: How could you experience the happiness of daily self-liberation if there were nothing left in you to overcome, nothing more to free?

Meaningful images such as these bring before us the mysterious wound in our soul and the inherited split in our consciousness. Our consciousness has been banished into the very nature we are called upon to take with us on our path to freedom. Only in this way can we also annul the division in our consciousness: by reconnecting matter and spirit in the daily creations of our thinking. Love in its soul has split into a state where self-love and love-of-the-other stand in opposition to one another, in order to give humanity the task, in freedom, of making the mutual support of these two a reality in an endless variety of ways.


## The downward and the upward path

The human being consists of body, soul, and spirit. In the body we experience the *imperatives* of nature. In our mind or spirit we are *free* to think creatively and act out of love. As soul we oscillate between these two worlds and experience the *tension* between unfreedom and freedom, between body and spirit. With its forces of love the soul can devote itself to both the bodily and the spiritual. It can take both the 'upward path' and the 'downward path'. It is precisely here that humanity has its freedom to choose.

Were a stable equilibrium to arise between these two great loves of the soul—between the body and the spirit—there would be no development. The strength the soul develops by seeking ever more self-determination in the direction it takes, will bring it forward and make it increasingly more akin and similar to the spirit. On the other hand, if the soul just passively lives out what the life of the body has to offer, it will develop an increasing inclination towards the world of matter and become progressively more entangled in its realm of necessity. To make development possible, the soul over the course of time has to decide ever more unequivocally, ever more definitively, which of the two, the one *or* the other, it will choose. Human beings experience themselves increasingly related either to everything spiritual or to the forces of nature. For the sake of freedom, their souls grow ever more fond either of the world of spirit or the world of matter.

In the first case, the soul looks with increasing decisiveness for the experiences of the spirit. The mind or spirit in turn has increasing success in understanding nature bit by bit through the soul, and progresses in spiritualizing nature and 'raising it up' to itself.

In the second case, the soul associates more and more strongly with bodily processes. This results in the human spirit becoming less and less able to master matter because the way is barred, so to speak, by strong bodily desires. The soul thus slowly forgets the spirit because it is increasingly satisfied with what the body has to offer. The human mind can end up in a condition where it is barely able to find its reflection in the soul anymore and cannot penetrate it properly. What is left is then just a self-centred ego with purely intellectual thinking, a lifeless reflection of sense-perceptions. We have then reached the imbalance that can often be observed in our materialistic age, in which many people live in almost exclusive surrender to the material world.

Just as the power of the human mind is able to permeate and enthuse the soul and give its own imprint to matter (we need only think of the achievements of science and technology,) so the world of matter, through its inherent inertia, can fill the soul with ever more cravings, dragging the spirit down and increasingly 'materializing' it. If human interest goes no further than the laws and processes of nature, if people orient their whole lives according to these, their minds will gradually lose the ability to do or be anything without the support of matter. Human beings can become so dependent on matter that its laws become *their* laws; they ultimately only experience the imperatives of nature, and in the end are justified in speaking of freedom as a mere illusion.

So-called materialism is no mere abstract theory: it is a very real and increasing dependence of the human mind on the immutable laws of matter. On this path, human thinking ultimately becomes just a reflection of external processes. What remains for the mind is then only dead images with which—as in modern science and technology—it can comprehend and dominate the aspect of the external world that is also dead. Even Immanuel Kant maintained that the human being is not capable of comprehending the element of life. What the thus deadened and soulless human mind of modern times has been able to generate is only a world of machines and—bearing in mind our terrible machines of war—a world of death and destruction. The downward path makes people's souls more animal-like in their natural drives, and the mind ever more machine-like, more mechanical in its thinking. People will then start asking themselves whether computers can't think better than they can, since the Internet already 'knows' so much more than any human individual could ever know.

The opposite happens when every process of our 'incarnation', of the embodiment of the individual human spirit or I, plays a part in the redemption and liberation of the world of matter. This is what Christianity means when it speaks of the mystery of the 'resurrection of the flesh', of the transformation of being or 'transubstantiation' of all that is physical and bodily into the free human spirit.


## Feminine imagination and masculine drive to action

In a lecture on the 4 January 1922, Rudolf Steiner points out that love in a woman emanates primarily from imagination and is always trying to form pictures, whereas love in a man has more of a desire character, emphasizing the will rather than the feelings. It is precisely this difference in disposition that daily gives them the possibility of finding a new harmony in life.

It may be that many women today are less acquainted with their own soul and increasingly lose sight of the world of imagination which is their special contribution to the masculine world. Nevertheless, it is said that since time immemorial every woman has carried an ideal image in her soul of the human being, no matter how unconscious or buried it may be, and hopes to find it once more in every individual. The fact that the ideal person can be realized on this earth only gradually, and indeed is often only very sketchily present at all, is very clear to the woman and not even of such great importance, because the image of the human being she has in her soul is not impaired by it. She loves this image above all, it lives in her in all its beauty as a comprehensive *ideal* into which she weaves all her imagination. She is unable to make any compromises here, nor does she want to.

A man, by contrast, understands little or nothing of this mystery of perfected beauty because all his energies are directed towards realizing himself in externally-oriented activity. He experiences the pulse of the times in the achievements of industry, technology, transport, and finance. He is often keen to create something for a woman that is externally visible in the world. The man asks: What is the use of all these beautiful ideals if we have to remain so far behind them in the reality of tangible things? What counts for a man is what human beings create with their own hands. He loves 'success' that is also externally visible. With self-confidence he enjoys showing others what he has attained and achieved in this world; he likes to talk about development, by which he often means unlimited economic growth and the unstoppable progress of technology. He is proud of his calculating intellect and its increasing ability to dominate the world. He can move with lightning speed between thought and action, because he is only too glad to bypass the soul lying between them with its—for him—so cumbersome world of feelings. He often lives like a spirit without a soul, a cold intellect, and then again like a body without a soul through his energetic 'hands on' engagement with the material world.

And woman, who can neither live nor act without soul, too often seeks 'emancipation' or liberation from her loneliness by masculinizing her being. In gruelling competition with men, she feels compelled to be 'as good as a man' with the result that she often abandons the last vestige of femininity in her soul.

What is fully human in us lives on the one hand by the *eternal* aspect which the woman guards and protects in her imagination, and on the other hand by what is accomplished in the succession of time, what people make visible in freedom, in which the man sees his life and all his pride. In the act of reproduction, the man's seed drives out the old form-giving forces from the female ovum in order to make space for the new ones that the new-born brings with them. And the woman receives in her body the archetype of the human being that seeks to become flesh in her child. For nine months she bears in her womb the mystery of incarnation, the eternal pregnancy of her soul.

Thus the female soul is nourished by the archetypes of imagination, whereas the masculine mind strives day by day, piece by piece, to conquer the world. Woman wishes to preserve her supersensory treasure, the perfect image of the human being. In her soul, all matter aspires towards spirit; in her, spirit wants again and again to breathe soul and life into the world of matter.

# 3. Love and Death

## *Which One Will Win?*

## Love, death, and sexuality

People have always been aware of the mysterious link between sexuality, love, and death, and expressed this knowledge in myths and works of art. This triplicity encompasses all the realms of human life: sexuality, where the forces of nature hold sway that bring forth the body; love, where all the forces of the soul find their harmony; and death, without doubt the most incisive experience of the human spirit.

The recurring image of the Expulsion from 'Paradise', which we find in many cultures, attempts to portray nothing less than the gradual and initially unconscious process in human beings of connecting progressively more deeply with matter, with their body. The descent of humanity from our divine-spiritual home, so it is said, was accompanied by the gradual darkening of our consciousness. As long as humanity experienced itself as part of a spiritual world, it could not develop an independent self-awareness. Only complete immersion in the physical body, which separated human individuals from the rest of the world, made it possible for them to think and act independently, to sense themselves as a fully distinct being. However, they largely lost consciousness of their spiritual origin. To regain this, to reclaim it through their own strength without giving up their self-awareness, is both the destiny and calling of human beings.

In very ancient times, reproduction took place in a sleep-like condition without people being able to participate in it with their awareness. It happened in much the same way as many processes still occur in the body today without the participation of human consciousness. We need only think of digestion which, like reproduction, is a natural process. It is hard to imagine what it would be like if our stomach only worked at our command. It carries out tasks we are completely unaware of, and this is precisely what is required for healthy digestion. Only when there is a pain, when something is not quite right, do we notice we have a stomach at all. The problems begin the moment human consciousness appears on the scene.

Through the ever closer connection with the body, it came about that people became more aware of their sensual drives and sensations. And they didn't just experience them but could also recognize them as such. A new-born child or even an animal feels its body no less than an adult, but it does not interpret its sensations in the way adults do as a matter of course. It cannot reflect on its pleasure or pain, about heat and cold, and thus cannot take up a stance with regard to these or deal with them freely. An adult, however, *can* do this: they can say, 'Oh, how good I feel! I am fine, so I'll carry on like this.' Or they can say, 'No, I don't like this! I don't want to continue like this, I have to change something. The room's getting too cold, I'll close the window.'

If there was a stage in evolution when all humanity was at the level of childhood, when with regard to their consciousness all human beings were like small children, then the reproductive powers must have worked through human beings at that time without their being able to bring them to consciousness. Only in the course of development—as today in the course of a single life—must human consciousness have 'fallen' more and more into the reproductive forces so that people could deal with them with increasing consciousness and freedom. Only in this way was it possible for people to separate the forces of reproduction from their actual purpose in order to retain for themselves just the experience of pleasure.

When an action is carried out *consciously*, its value and meaning are essentially determined by the person's intention. Also in procreation human thoughts began to play an increasingly decisive role. Parents are finding it more and more difficult to simply accept having children without first planning for it out of their free will. Previously people said, 'Children are a gift from God,' and perhaps there are many who still say so today. But in their thoughts, with regard to their family planning, there are perhaps some parents who would rather God hadn't been quite so 'fulsome' in his generosity.

Forces are at work in the act of procreation that are oriented towards procreation by their very nature, but today it is largely left to the free will of the individual how they are used. By nature, the sexual forces act 'unselfishly' because they serve to help another human being to a life on earth. But if a person wants to enjoy the strong lust that these forces

44

produce, while excluding procreation, they then use in an 'egotistical' way, purely for themself, what nature gives to serve the embodiment of another human being.

Dealing with sexual forces is thus always connected with a decision to give life or to refuse life. The sexual act can be both an act of deepest love, making it possible for a human being to incarnate, and an act of total self-love and self-pleasure. Self-love is the unavoidable starting-point of love, but human beings only develop further when they increasingly 'expand' this self-love to love more and more people as they love themselves. If sex drive enables a radical form of self-love, then it is the greatest challenge in itself to overcome one-sided self-love. The power of love is the strongest power that can defeat the greatest egotism.

People can abuse their bodies in various ways—including eating and drinking, sleeping and waking—which naturally causes them to suffer both emotionally and mentally because their most precious instrument is made less serviceable thereby. If people alienate the reproductive forces from their purpose, this cannot remain without profound effect on their whole being. The destiny of human development towards freedom and love is decided to a great extent in this area.


## Death as the gift of love

Human beings experience perhaps the deepest darkening of their consciousness when, in their thinking, they expect to find the highest level of freedom and love where, in fact, these are completely lacking. Only a deeply 'fallen' thinking can regard the experience of the highest degree of self-centredness, absorption in the drives of one's own body, as the expression of true love. The essence of the human being is our thinking consciousness. The deepest level of 'fall' can only be a condition of consciousness that is no longer able to distinguish between good and evil, that no longer knows what makes us more loving and free, and what does not. A state of thinking that mixes up love and egotism can be called 'tragic'. No one, who in their *thinking* takes what is wrong to be what is right, can steer their life in the right direction.

This begs the question: What is the meaning of death, of leaving the body behind?

A person who couldn't die would increasingly identify themself with their body, would become totally isolated from other beings and incapable of any empathy for others because they themself would lack the experience of what they are apart from their body. A person who couldn't die would experience only what is determined through the body. The soul had to connect more and more deeply with the body in the course of evolution so that man could really experience himself as an independent being. But this connection should not go so far that the individual becomes fully engrossed in the experience of the body. In order to give human beings the possibility of experiencing themselves as spirit, the gift of death was given, the possibility of leaving the body for a period in order to regain in a spiritual world the certainty that each of us is a spirit among spirits.

Two opposite experiences demonstrate the connection between love, sexuality, and death: these are sense-perception on the one hand, and sexual pleasure of the body on the other. Every percept requires the instrument of the body. From birth we construct a body that makes the world perceptible to us from various points of view. Every percept is a challenge to us to find its corresponding concept through our thinking. Through thinking we recognize our connection with the world, we can see ever better our common origin with it. Our bodily senses are like gateways to the world that enable a never-ending tension between self-love and love-for-others, between life in the body and life in the world.

We find the exact opposite in the pleasure of the sexual forces that excludes procreation. Here self-love is not experienced as the necessary prerequisite to love for others—in the striving of both for balance—but excludes love for the one that is seeking to incarnate. If death had not arisen in the course of evolution, if human beings could never experience themselves as a purely spiritual being, they would, through the temptation of one-sided bodily pleasure, gradually fall into complete self-love, because this operates with the imperative of nature. Love for the world and for other people, on the other hand, only comes from freedom, and can therefore always also be omitted.

Thus the so-called Fall can be understood as a fall into separation through the body. It is not awareness of this separation that is not good, since experiencing oneself as an individual being through the body is the necessary prerequisite for freedom. Human beings become 'un-good' and therefore unhappy when, out of freedom, they fail to win through to love for others in addition to their nature-given self-love. They can only be happy when their bodies do not one-sidedly serve their own pleasure alone, but self-love and love-for-others equally.

A body filled with mineral substance only ever allows a limited exchange between egotism and altruism, since two people can only become completely one if they are able to 'penetrate' each other entirely, so to speak. But matter does not allow penetration and thus prevents the perfect union of two people. They can have a similar standpoint in their convictions, but in the physical world—bodily, in other words—it is quite impossible for them to stand on the same spot, to have one 'standpoint' together.

The goal of all evolution for the forces of love can therefore only be progressively to 'spiritualize' the body, thus dematerializing it in order to liberate it from its impenetrable elements. Only in this way is living simultaneously in oneself and in the other possible. As hard as it is for a materialistic thinking to imagine, self-love and love-for-others become one when an individual can live as much in another person as in themself. If the goal of human evolution is the spiritualization of all our bodily nature, and if this spiritualization is only achieved through the work of each individual on their complete liberation from matter, then it is obvious that such an evolution requires long periods of time for which a single life and a single death would in no way suffice. But it is ominous, indeed even tragic, when people fail to recognize the true direction of development, when they not only approve of shutting themselves off in bodily pleasure—the dead-end of evolution—but even intensify it.


## Don't say 'I love you' too hastily

The body is the precipitate of all a person's needs; that is why it is also the place of great opposites, of all the things that are mutually exclusive. The plate of food that satisfies my hunger cannot at the same time satisfy the hunger of one who sits opposite me. No one could imagine that by satisfying their own appetite they are satisfying the needs of another, or that they love another just because they are sitting together and eating at the same table. In sexual life, on the other hand, the impression can easily arise that one loves another when one uses their body to give pleasure and enjoyment to oneself.

We might ask ourselves here whether we should not also put in a good word for our 'first love', as was done in the text above. Why should it not be possible, when my self-love demands the satisfaction of my sex drive, not to add to it a love for the satisfaction of the sex drive of the other? After all: love thy neighbour as thyself. This question can only be answered by looking more closely at the fact that selfishness is always accompanied by a certain self-deception.

Let's assume that a man is an arch-egotist when it comes to money, that the more money he can pile up the happier he feels. But one day a desire awakens in him to make sure that his fellow human beings also get money. What is the result? He starts paying more attention to the financial concerns of others, he also takes care of their assets. Perhaps he has the notion to try stocks and shares on the stock exchange. But sooner or later it will become evident to him how the stock market works: a small number of people can only get more money by many others losing it. He will make the discovery that it is only possible for everyone to benefit, without exception, if everyone overcomes their greed for money, and instead develops more and more a sense of community. This would probably result in a reduction of his own fortune over time, but also in a corresponding increase in his joy in the love of others.

It is in the nature of the thing that if you are oriented towards others, are involved in their concerns and engaged in their well-being, you acquire a whole new way of thinking and living. By means of mutual support and well-intentioned concern, any kind of one-sided egotism is gradually stripped away. One can't love others as oneself by putting two egotisms side by side unaltered, or even adding them together. Mutual love is only possible when each party overcomes their egotism more and more.

A Persian tale tells of a young man who goes on a pilgrimage to a shrine. On his way he meets a monk and accompanies the monk some of the way and shares meals with him. Before they bid each other farewell, the young man asks the monk his name. Very hesitantly the monk tells him he is the Angel of Death. 'Then tell me, when will I die?' the young man wants to know. The angel answers, 'You will die on your wedding night.'

After this, to everyone's surprise, the young man refuses all prospects of marriage until at the urging of his old parents he finally reveals his secret. They try to allay his fears, give him good advice and persuade him to have no worries about marrying because when the time comes and the Angel of Death appears, they will step forward in their son's place and give their old souls to the angel. They finally manage to convince their son, who by now was thirty years old, to find a wife.

When the wedding night approaches, and the bride and groom take each other's hand, the Angel of Death does indeed appear. The young man's father is called and doesn't hesitate to offer his soul as promised. But when the angel had pulled his soul out up to his chest, he changes his mind and says we would rather keep his soul after all. Then the young man's mother rushes in to give her soul to the angel, but when he has pulled her soul out as far as her neck, she too regrets her sacrifice and likewise wishes to undo it. Finally the bride steps forward. 'I will not be guilty of bringing misfortune to my bridegroom,' she says to the Angel of Death, 'so take me.' But just when the Angel of Death has pulled her soul out up to her nose, the voice of God sounds out: 'Leave them both in peace. As reward for the bride's willingness to sacrifice herself, I give this couple thirty years of life together!'

The mystery of the indissoluble bond between love, sexuality, and death is expressed in a wonderful way in the images of this tale. In order not to die for love, another death is required: human beings must sacrifice themselves, must rid themselves of all their egotisms. The unfree drive of instinct loses its dominant power as soon as one turns one's attention to another. As Diotima said to Socrates: first you fall in love with the body of the other, then you learn to love the warmth of their soul, and finally the light of their mind or spirit. The soul death to which bodily lust leads us can be transformed by the soul into an inner re-birth through love of the spirit.

What has always been known as the 'path of purification'—and which today's materialism often derides as something that simply prevents people from enjoying 'the best that life has to offer', meaning the enjoyments of the senses—actually seeks to be nothing less than the path of love. It is the aspiration to make the other not the instrument of our own ego-centred desires, but the goal of our devoted love. Purifying oneself through love for others does not mean frantically suppressing our drives or scourging ourselves into alienation from the world. Rather it means wanting to *understand* our drives for what they are in reality, and what effects they have not only in ourselves but in the other when they remain unpurified. It means wanting to free ourselves more and more from everything that makes us unfree, thus permitting us to meet the one we love in the freedom of love.


## 'I love you because I can't live without you'

The soul is the wellspring of all wishes, the body is the source of all needs. The soul seeks to meet the soul of the other, whereas the body cannot but remain enclosed in itself. As free spirits, two people can become completely one by virtue of the knowledge that each can attain of the other.

Man seeks his own soul in woman, albeit only semi-consciously, without wishing to lose his power of intellectual thinking; and woman seeks for the thinking spirit in man, without having to surrender her soul-warmth in the process. In this mutual embrace of woman and man, of soul and spirit, the original Adam can come to life once more, who was both male and female. In this union, eternity, which makes woman woman, becomes one with time, which makes man man as he progresses from one achievement to the next.

The question arises here as to whether love is really something immortal. True love can never die—so says the woman's heart that would like to live in what is eternal. The thought that her love could die one day, scares her. Today love is my all, she says to herself, and could a day come when it no longer exists?

Because everything of a bodily nature must die sooner or later, only the aspect of love that is restricted to the body can die. But nothing in the human being has to stay restricted to the body. Because love is an aspect of everything immortal, an immortal love can 'embody' itself in the body. When I love the soul and spirit in myself and in the other, I make my love immortal like our souls, eternal like our spirit.

All experiences we have through the body are 'made human' when they are absorbed by the soul and spirit. The same happens to percepts when thinking finds the eternal idea in them. All things can be spiritualized in this way, liberated from their transitory nature, and 'incorporated' into an eternal nature. Thus love too can overcome everything in it of a transitory nature, and thus itself become imperishable. Every person is immortal to the extent that they think and love everything that never dies.

What does a person do, who throughout their life has had needs that can be satisfied almost solely through the body, when they die and no longer have a body? The food instinct serves to maintain the body and keep it healthy; it exists while the body is there and ceases with death. But the gourmet whose favourite activity is eating and drinking, has cravings that go beyond just those necessary for maintaining the body, and have little to do with health. These do not originate from the body but from the soul.

The body is no longer there after death; but the soul certainly is—along with all those desires which, because a body is required to satisfy them, can no longer be satisfied. There is no alternative for the deceased but to consume themself in longing. They have to burn away all their body-related desires in order to be released from the terrible suffering that arises because the desires can no longer be satisfied. All religions speak unanimously of the flames of 'purgatory' which cleanse the souls of the deceased from all desires that require the body. What applies to the friends of good cuisine applies no less to those for whom sex is the all-important thing in life.

When a person aspires to that which never passes away, when they love the soul and spirit in all people above everything else, they will feel immortal in their love. And after their death, in the realm of souls and spirits, they will be able to experience their love far more strongly and blissfully. One who lives in this way no longer fears death, since fear of death only shows that one is at the very beginning of the long path to love. Love is made immortal to the extent that we are able to love what is immortal in every human being above all else.


## Love that knows no death

Every person who has a superabundance of the forces of love, enough not only for self-love but also for love of others, has these forces by virtue of all the individuals who have made their development possible. Each of us can only love as much as we ourselves are loved by others. For every person who is rich in loving forces there were many others who gave them the opportunity to advance in their development. Whenever someone attains a faculty, they owe this to the fact that there are others who in some way forgo this attainment for themselves, quite irrespective of whether the sacrifice is made consciously or unconsciously. One who is able to love a great deal has already received the reward for their love, they have experienced in the past the love that now enables them to love in turn. True love is always experienced as reciprocal love, it is inseparable from gratitude. Those who truly love know that they only want to give back in their love what they themselves have by virtue of the renunciation of others in past times.

Those in a relationship who think they love more than their friend, or who complain that they feel exploited by the egotism of the other, might ask themselves: If I can really love more than the other, how did I get these forces of love? The person who today demands more love from me than they can give, is perhaps demanding back the love they once bestowed on me in a distant past. One who is able to love greatly is a great debtor. This, in turn, is one of love's mysteries: the lover sees in the beloved a former lover, and in the beggar for love, one who has given away all their love to the lover.

In 'pity' for the other's neediness in matters of love, the lover, even if often only unconsciously, feels a longing in themself to give back to the other the love-forces that belong to them, because in the past the other gave more to the lover than they received. One of the most beautiful images in the Christian Gospels is the Washing of the Feet, where it says that Christ bowed down in his love to his disciples and washed their feet. He does this in gratitude, and expressly tells them that he could never have become a teacher if there were no disciples, he could never have become the Saviour of humankind if there were no people in need of redemption, and yearning for it.

Every mother's love is, if lived more deeply, also a requited love, because every mother owes her motherhood to her child. Those who seek the reward for their love in being loved, are still needy, are beggars for love; but those, on the other hand, who find the reward of love in loving, are rich in love. The happiness of those who feel loved is transitory; the love that is able to bestow itself, on the other hand, does not pass away. One who lives in love lives all the time in eternity. One who loves little, needs the success of earthly deeds for their feeling of self-worth. One who loves much experiences in their love the enduring 'success' of all earthly evolution.

In a relationship between two people, one is always more attentive and loving than the other. This is the one who can better understand that certain difficulties can only be overcome if they bring more love into the relationship than perhaps the other is able to give. They will be able to say to themself: Perhaps I owe my powers of love above all to those who now long for it most, who are now completely dependent on it. Those who meet someone who is in the fortunate position of being able to love more, may long to have some of this love because they themselves once contributed to its development.

Each of us can only give what we have, and everything we have is something we once received—not directly from a god who sits on a throne above the clouds but by way of our encounters with other people. No one is rich in love who had not been given this wealth by all humanity, by being able to share in an abundance of beauty and good that comes from all and is meant for all. The stomach's relationship to the kidney is no different, and vice versa: every organ gets everything it needs from the organism, and in turn gives it back.

One who is thankful that they are able to love deeply will never feel exploited, even when the other, who perhaps is not able to love so much, takes advantage. It is one of the open secrets of love that it cannot be exploited. If a mother in her generosity gives her thirty-year-old son access to her bank account, and he shamelessly 'exploits' her, she might perhaps intervene quickly and put a stop to it. But if she is full of love, she will do this not because she feels exploited but because her son is *harming himself* by doing this. It is *for his sake* that she will prevent any further supposed exploitation. If it were good for his further development, she would gladly go on allowing herself to be 'exploited'.

A young mother with small children, who is lucky enough to be brimming over with forces of love, would on no account tolerate it if her husband never lifted a finger in the household. Not, however, because this makes her feel exploited, but because she cannot bear to see the person she loves harming himself with his egotism—which would ultimately also have a bad effect on the children. Another mother in a similar situation might indeed feel exploited (this is very probable and only human) but it only means that her love has not yet reached the stage of 'unexploitability'.

And the amazing thing is that a person who feels exploited in their love will find it harder to set boundaries for the 'exploiter' than someone who doesn't feel used. The latter is less concerned about their own feelings than about the well-being of the loved one. Their strong love gives them the strength to be relentless if this is for the good of the other. A person, on the other hand, who feels exploited, unconsciously senses that they want to set boundaries to the egotism of the other only for their own sake. And because their love is not yet perfect, they often cannot find the strength to remain unyielding. An individual who is strict in their treatment of the other for their own sake, will easily be plagued by pricks of conscience. But a bad conscience such as this will immediately have the effect of challenging us to develop ourselves further. True love can never give us a bad conscience because it is itself the good conscience of the human being.

True love enjoys being 'beneficial'; it can only become more enriched by it. The more others make use of it, the richer the love becomes, and the more 'beneficial' it makes itself. An exploitation in the sense of consuming something or using it up entirely, is quite out of the question in this situation. An egotist always harms themself, but they cannot harm the love of another. 'But the other is making my life difficult; this can't go on,' someone might object. We can answer by saying: If you think the other is making your life difficult, this can only mean that you can develop the forces of your love further.

The more opportunities love can find to bestow itself, the more it becomes 'full of love' and the less it needs to give itself sparingly or to think of itself as scarce. Those who truly love know that the self-centredness of others can only give their own love the chance to grow. Objectively speaking no one can do evil to a lover because love is the power that transforms all evil in the world into good. One who has the power from the depths of their heart to love even someone who exploits them, only strengthens their love, they truly make it undying. Someone who exploits another's love is most in need of it. And one who truly loves will want to love that person most of all. We can give more love to someone who needs more love than to someone who themself is able to love deeply.

And how much suffering is love able to bear? It is another mystery of love that each person's capacity for compassion is only as great as their capacity to suffer. The forces of love are generated through suffering, and one who truly loves is no less grateful for suffering than for love. Suffering is sacred to one who loves because it is what enables a person to love in the first place. How can love complain about suffering when everything love is and is able to do, is by virtue of suffering? One who loves knows about this mystery of the inseparability of suffering and love, and does not demand from someone, who perhaps has suffered less, more than they are able to give. A person's moral weight is their capacity to love, and their love has the weight of their capacity to suffer. And it is not the person who has suffered hard external blows of fate who has more capacity for suffering, but the one who, even with an outwardly peaceful life, completely internalizes the suffering of others, is able to make it entirely their own. If a young person experiences much suffering due to cancer, not all their friends will be able to empathize with them in the same way. One friend might perhaps remain inwardly indifferent, another might feel deep compassion, each according to their capacity to suffer and to love.

The more one who loves can accompany in their heart the concerns of other people, the stronger their love becomes and the deeper their gratitude. A person who is grateful for the suffering bestowed on them, will never seek a suffering that is more or less or different from that which the wisdom of destiny brings to meet them. Love knows that only a wisdom greater than human wisdom knows the right amount of suffering for each individual. One who has experienced the blessing of suffering knows that they can transform all suffering into undying love, into the most precious pearl of the earthly world that itself is nothing less than crystallized, purified suffering.


## Thoughts, words, and deeds of love

The experience of love is always accompanied by the experience of death and new beginning. We cannot love without choosing, and choosing always means going without something else. Every time we leave something behind, we inwardly die a little: a part of us remains behind, a part that belonged to us or could have belonged to us.

Above all in the sphere of the body love has to choose again and again, because everything of a bodily nature is exclusive. If a woman chooses a man to be the father of her child, she has to exclude all other men in this regard, she has to renounce all other men as a father for her child. The *deeds of love* that I perform with my hands are usually directed to only a few people. Others will not be directly affected by my actions. And these actions only serve the people in my closer circle while they are alive. I cannot give a deceased one a kiss, I cannot prepare a good meal for them, cannot go to the theatre with them.

One who in daily life expresses their love by acts for which their body is the tool, has to forgo doing this simultaneously for others. But they will be a great treasure to those whom they accompany in life and who in turn choose to accompany them. This love that is expressed in actions becomes undying by what it pours into the hearts of others and by what it thus spiritualizes through them.

Acts of love 'embody' love in the here and now, in space and time. *Thoughts of love* do not recognize such boundaries. In thinking, love can reach all people, all worlds. And the most beautiful way to love another is to think of them as what they wish to become, to recognize them in their true being, and to try to understand their actions in this light, which perhaps are not always perfect.

If in my love for another I serve through my thoughts what they in turn are to others, then through this other I love all people. This is a love that sees each individual as part of a far greater whole composed of the uniqueness of all people who cannot be different from how they are. Each one belongs to the whole and serves it in their own special way, as each organ in the human body belongs to and serves the whole organism. Those who comprehend and love another in their uniqueness, love the whole of humanity through them. At death, only the external acts of love cease. All the thoughts and feelings of love which gave those acts life, endure on both this and the far side of the threshold of death, they are immortal like the human being from whom they stem.

*Words of love* are a bridge between thoughts and deeds. If in its deeds love creates a body, if, in thinking, human beings recognize themselves as spirit, then words facilitate conversation between soul and soul. Which of us does not know the healing power of a loving word? Words of forgiveness, of comfort, of empowerment. How courageous loving words can make us, and how happy! Loving words can become a precious treasure that the soul of the loved one never loses. A person who, if only once, really felt loved in their life, will not be able to forget this love in all eternity.

# Wonder, compassion, and conscience: thrice-immortal love

From roughly the sixth pre-Christian century onwards, three new faculties emerge in humanity that are closely connected with the incarnation of the Being who is itself Love, and who at that time was preparing his appearance on earth. The faculty of *wonder* appeared in early Greek philosophy; the teaching of *compassion* was brought by Buddha to Indian culture; and the power of *conscience*, of morality, was the great contribution of Hebrew culture.

The Greeks were the first to point out that the origin of philosophy, the love of wisdom, lies in the power of wonder. And this indeed is so because the world can only be understood by one in whom it can create a sense of wonder. The genius of [the German] language comes to our aid here: <u>*Verwunderung*</u> (= wonder, amazement) at the phenomena of the world changes into <u>*Bewunderung*</u> (= admiration, veneration) that sees wonders all around it. To love the world means to see it with the amazed eye of a child. For a child, everything is full of wonder, is wonderfully beautiful, is wonderful [*wundervoll, wunderschön, wunderbar*]. The 'adult child' can take what is full of wonder in the world into their thinking, the wondrously beautiful into their feeling, and the wonderful into their willing, and thus perform the threefold wonder of love in their actions.

Love never ceases to be amazed at the beloved, is open every day to new surprises, always ready for new discoveries. The ability to wonder generates heartfelt interest, interest increases our attention, and attention is the inexhaustible source of love's moral imagination. Only those who can be amazed at things are able to understand the world and people with increasing depth; they perceive things beyond themselves so to speak. Plato still knew that in each of us there lives a memory of everything we experienced in a purely spiritual world before birth, before we entered into the physical body. There we did not live outside of other beings, not outside of things, but were one with them, perceived ourselves as living amongst them.

The physical senses cause people on earth to perceive a world that they encounter, a world that appears to be outside themselves. Every sense-perception is an experience of alienation from the world, it seems to indicate a distance between the human being and things; it challenges our thinking to form concepts in order to immerse ourselves in the inside of things. Thinking changes every perception into a spiritual spark that enables the world, piece by piece, to light up again in the human mind. The whole world literally lights up for the human being in thinking.

The child of Raphael's *Sistine Madonna* comes to mind: the child, carried on his mother's arm, in whose enigmatic eyes this whole astonishment, almost fright, comes to expression—at a world that has become separated from humanity and now, with everything that happens in it, seems to be external to the human being. No wonder children never tire of hearing fairy tales. The world of fairy tales is a world full of wonders and the child is more and more astonished and calls out, 'Granny, tell is *again*!' It is not so long ago that they descended from the wide expanse of heaven, and therefore still have a strong need to submerse themselves in this world again and again.

At the same time as the ancient Greeks were speaking of wonder as the beginning of philosophy, Buddha brought to the Orient the profound teaching of compassion and love. He awoke the awareness in humanity that all suffering can only be overcome by compassion. The essence of Buddhism lies in this highest of moral challenges. And its fulfilment came a few centuries later when the Being who is full of love brought to humanity the active forces of love. The significance of Christianity does not lie in some kind of theory, but in the most comprehensive deed of love that has ever been performed on the earth. The essential thing in Christianity is the essence of love itself, it is its love that enlightens people's minds, warms their hearts, and gives energy to their deeds.

In wonder, human beings love through their thinking mind or spirit; in compassion they love with spirit and soul; in their moral responsibility towards the earth and others, in the conscientiousness of their actions, they love with spirit, soul, and body. Spiritual love incarnates through human hands in their good deeds.

The fact that it was possible for a moral conscience to develop in the individual human being, is due to the particular contribution to humanity of the Hebrew people, a contribution made as preparation for the Messiah, the great evolutionary ideal of all humanity. This people of monotheism, of the religion of the One God, is the nation that in an exemplary way was able to develop the forces of the individual I, an I that is strong enough to accept moral responsibility for its own deeds.

In ancient times there was not yet even a word by which individual conscience could be named. The god of the Jews, Yahweh, already points in his name to the dignity of the individual person. Yahweh means roughly 'I am'. The Yahweh-individual says to themself: I am an I, I am the same for myself over the course of time, I am the same person I was yesterday, that I am today, and I will still be the same tomorrow. The consequences of my actions can work back on me because my I-consciousness continues to exist. I sense in myself the will to accept responsibility for my deeds and actions.

Love means going beyond oneself, overcoming the isolation we experience in our own personal needs, in order to orientate ourselves towards others. The working of love in the world takes three paths: the path of *thinking*, the path of the *heart*, and the path of *conscience*. In cognition through wonderment it is the spirit that loves; in compassion, human beings love with their soul; in conscientious action, love permeates the whole body and makes human beings what they always wish to be: love incarnate.

## Death is a transition, love is a new beginning

Death is not an objective reality; it is an illusion of human consciousness. What is real is only the fear of death in the body-bound soul because it fears that, along with the body, it too will pass away with all the thoughts and ideals that live in it. But this fear also performs an important function: through fear of death, human beings become aware that the body-free life of their spirit after death will not be just a gift of nature but something won through the effort of their freedom. What remains for every person after death is as much of soul and spirit as they were able to gain in life through their freedom. Immortality is not immediate immortality—only as much of each human soul remains after death as has loved, and only as much of each human mind as has thought creatively. Only love can make the soul immortal, and a great love makes a rich and gregarious life after death possible. Nothing that lives in the human heart can be lost; it all survives death unscathed.

According to the sacred scriptures of all religions, human beings at the beginning of their evolution felt at home in the spiritual world even during their earthly existence. The initial tentative encounter with matter could not yet alienate people from the spirit. And death did not yet evoke this terrible fear of falling into a bottomless nothingness, because throughout their lives people could maintain contact with spiritual beings and with those who had died. They knew from experience that death signifies little more than a change in location. For someone who died, it was as though they left this place only to emerge in another very close by.

Just imagine we were not the hard-boiled materialists of the present day. Suppose we didn't live with the usual modern belief that our entire inner world—knowledge, love, morality—is just an effluvium of the physical brain. And then imagine that we are people for whom thoughts and feelings can exist without the body, for whom stones, plants, animals, and the whole glorious world of the senses are indeed real, but for whom the thoughts and deeds of love and everything else a person does out of freedom, are much more real. Imagine further that we could experience ourselves as an eternal spirit that clothed itself only temporarily in bodily substance in order to practise on earth the skill and art of love, and which then laid the bodily envelope aside in order to harvest the fruits of that love in the spiritual. If this were the case, what would death signify for such a person? It would only be the transition from one joyful experience to another.

And what would a person who experiences things in this way say to themselves as they crossed the threshold of death? They would say: 'I have spent a few years on the earth in a body composed of matter, and therefore could have a life of only short duration … I felt a bit heavy and constrained in that body … Here above, where I am bodiless, I feel a good deal lighter and freer … But it was a good challenge, in the cramped world of the earth down there below with all its unfreedoms and constraints, to assert oneself as a free spirit! And the love I was able to give on earth is certainly very different from the love we experience here above … What makes earthly love so beautiful is that it is attained through suffering, is won from suffering … Because of this, the love I have brought with me from there below gives me even more joy than it did during life. But look how the people down there are weeping for me! They think I'm dead … If only they knew!'

Death is the great delusion of our 'fallen' consciousness, a consciousness that no longer knows the immortal reality of love. The loveless person's fear of having to live without love after death is justified. Only an individual in whom love is dead for everything supersensory and eternal can speak of death as a true reality. Love of the spirit is the gateway to the world of spirit; only by this love will human beings liberate themselves. What a person loves is forever anchored in their heart. The deeper a person loves, the stronger they experience what is immortal in them.

## Is it possible ever to lose someone we love?

When we separate or part company, it can sometimes seem that the other has disappeared from our life for ever. When two people live a great distance apart, the distance has meaning only when looked at purely externally. But people are a great deal more than just their bodies consisting of visible matter. Thus we can all ask: What of the other stays with me in my inner being after our separation or parting? To this question we can all answer: What stays with me is all the love I have for them. If 'love' also disappears at parting, this does not mean that love is transitory but rather that it was never there in the first place.

Love that is really there never ceases to exist. It is the nature of love that it can never die. Love cannot give notice; even at a spatial distance it cannot but remain true to itself. One of the strongest experiences of love we can have is when we are distant from the loved one, when they are far away from us in body. Our longing for them can make them present for us far more strongly than if they were physically here. When a person is consumed with the longing of love, the loved one is present in them—and how!

Seen purely externally, death is the most decisive form of separation. At the same time it is a challenge to those left behind to keep the deceased one alive in their hearts. Those who leave us through their death deprive us of their visible aspect in the hope that they will thereby be present in our soul even more strongly than was possible when they were in the body. At death, life next to one another comes to an end, and a life in one another can begin. Before their death, the loved one lived beside me, after their death they can live in me. It is beautiful when we have those we love around us; it is even more beautiful if, before death and after it, we can carry them in our heart.

And how could the one left behind, who had loved the deceased for a lifetime, do other than feel happy for them? At the death of a friend, a person who remains shut in themself is overcome by a boundless grief because they miss the beloved. This is understandable. It is human. But it is not the expression of perfect love. The tears that are wept for a deceased one are tears of self-love. We feel alone, as though deserted by the person who filled the place at our side. As contradictory as it may sound, it is nevertheless true that the stronger love becomes, the more it succeeds in experiencing joy with one who, having fulfilled their life's task, has only seemingly left the earth, and who can only be saddened by the sorrow of those left behind. One who finds the strength to feel joy with the deceased one, makes the joy perfect on both sides.

Living with those that have died means striving to love as they love. They can certainly love better than the living because their consciousness is far brighter; they have left behind all the boundaries of the visible world, a world full of self-centredness and self-love. They now know what dying means: it means transforming all egotism, bit by bit, into pure love.

The dead speak to the living constantly. Spiritually they are always with them and have an infinite amount to tell them. It is the fault of those left behind if they do not hear these words. Many people today are so materialistically-minded that for them it is as though the deceased do not exist. It seems as though the so-called dead are mute, whereas in reality it is the so-called living who have become deaf.

People make their love immortal by learning to converse in the language of the spirit with their beloved deceased. It is as though the deceased were ceaselessly playing a melody or a song on the four strings of a special violin, as though in this way they wished to communicate intensively to the living the four ways in which the deceased live.

The first string is about becoming one:

> *'I feel one with all beings,*
> *I have overcome all separation.'*

For the living, love is the striving to remove all separation, and for the dead distance and separation no longer exist. In the spiritual world all beings are interwoven in one another.

The second string is about gratitude:

> *'I live in gratitude*
> *and thank everyone and everything.'*

Living on the other side of death means to comprehend what each of us owes every other person whom our destiny has allowed us to meet. The dead live in the sure knowledge that everything they are has been bestowed on them, that every human spirit owes what it has been able to become, to the whole world. And they rejoice at the prospect of every-thing they will give back in the future.

The third string is about trust:

> *'I look to the future, full of trust.'*

Thus the dead sing, for they know now that every human being can only evolve further if they help others—in a world that offers each of us the best for what we need in our advancement. The deceased live in mutual trust and in trust to us who have remained behind on the earth. They have insight into the destinies of humanity and know that human love is the meaning of the earth.

The fourth melody sounds out on the fourth string:

> *'The love I experience here above*
> *makes me younger and younger.'*

The same time that in its course causes the living in their bodies to grow ever older, causes the dead in their love to grow ever younger. And this too is one of the wonders of love: when the living cultivate a conversa-tion of love with the deceased, they are able to partake more and more of the deceased's love, a love which, even during life on earth, can make the human heart grow young as the body grows old. At the age of 80 we can encounter life as openly as a small child, with eyes full of amazement, with a soul full of wonder.

Living well means making love so strong that it can transform every death into a resurrection of the spirit. The deceased's four messages of love can awaken four kinds of love in the living:

- love for death
- love for daily dying
- love for the dying
- love for the dead.

Francis of Assisi called death his brother. This was an intuition of genius with regard to love, for only one who sees in death the crowning of life, the coming to life in a world of light and love, can love death as a brother.

Those who can regard death with gratitude will also be able to love dying daily. Where consciousness and love unfold their power, they feed on the physical organism. It is sad to have to grow older without simultaneously expanding one's consciousness and deepening one's love. But it is the greatest happiness of life to thank advancing age and the increasing frailty of the body for a constantly expanding consciousness and an ever deeper love.

Those for whom death and daily dying have become dear, will also be able to hold the elderly in their heart who are preparing for their death. Every dying person who is preparing themself for the last consecration of life in order to enter the spiritual world, deserves the deepest love.

After death, the deceased experiences the destructive effects of self-love and the beneficial effects of their love. Daily conversation with those who have died can become a schooling in love where the one living on the earth learns to purify self-love in the crucible of love for the other. And love for those who have passed on will be able to make earthly love ever richer and richer.

# 4. Love and Reason

*The Heart's Logic is Different*

## The intellect's laws of thought and the motives of the heart

Logic and love relate to each other like head and heart in the human being. Among the most beautiful things in life are the thousand sparks produced by the inner tension that is always present between the clever thoughts of the head and the wise intimations of the heart. The head's logic wants to find a logical reason for every action a person performs, but the heart has its own motives that are usually very different from those of the intellect. The 'whys and wherefores' of the heart never depend on a thin thread like that of logic, but rise from the depths of life-experience, from realms in which the intellect by itself cannot get very far.

Everyone lives in this beneficial field of tension between thought and feeling, between deliberation and experience. People feel unhappy when one side threatens to suppress the other, when there is an inner imbalance. This can even lead to physical illness since the actual cause of illness is never in the body, in purely material processes; our body always expresses things that have occurred beforehand in our soul or mind.

In the matter of the intellect and love, over a long period people regarded the intellect as an aspect of men, and sought the forces of the heart in women. While no one would view this in such a one-sided way today—the many gradations and exceptions being too apparent—there is nevertheless a distinct tendency in men towards dry, intellectual thinking, whereas for many women the forces of the heart are more important than the intellect. Consciously or unconsciously, every human being strives for the healthy harmony of all their forces; only in the interplay of what the mind demands of us and where the heart seeks to lead us, does each of us ultimately find happiness. It is a matter of gaining a better knowledge of when to incline more towards the deliberations of reason, and when to give the heart the leading role. We cannot say that one is more important or better than the other; each side plays an indispensable part in human happiness. There are no two people in whom the capacities of love and reason, of devotion and cleverness, are distributed in equal measure, for each person's inner balance is also constantly changing.

It is precisely this mutable interplay of inner forces that makes every meeting, every relationship between people, so fascinating. What makes the love between two people particularly valuable is precisely the possibility each has to give the other what is less developed in that other. If the balance between the forces of the intellect and the heart were not constantly changing, if there were no deficiencies, no vacillations, no disturbances—there would be no more development. Fortunately, there is no one who is 'unemployed' in this manner, for they would lack what is most beautiful in life: being always on the move every day to conjure up a new equilibrium in our forces.

A person in whom the forces of the heart predominate might have difficulty in seeing the importance for life of thinking. However, wherever it is a matter of classifying the world's phenomena in everyday life in an unbiased and objective manner so as to be able to orient ourselves accordingly, logical thinking is indispensable. No one can expect the world to organize itself around them, but everyone can require of themselves that they be directed by the world according to their situation in life. In order to do this, each of us must be able to gain an increasing understanding of the world in its objective reality, which can only be attained by intellect and reason, by the objectivity of a scientifically trained thinking.

For someone oriented toward the heart, the meaning of many of their encounters in life lies in being stimulated by others to discover the importance of the intellect. In their feelings they tend to ask what the point is of all these dry theories. We get much farther with the heart's warmth, so they maintain. But this is precisely why destiny leads them again and again to encounters with people who say to them: 'You know what, I really can't do much with your warm love that makes you so happy. If you really want to help me, try to get your head working as well! You can't say you love me unless you also try to *understand* who I am. Your sentimentality alone achieves absolutely nothing. The best thing would be if you could look at things objectively with cool reason.' A rational person is naturally not always terribly sensitive in how they treat heart-people. Sensitivity is not their strong point. Nevertheless, destiny treats every gushy dreamer with particular love when it brings them into contact with head-people. And a heart-person will be grateful for this help in experiencing the happiness of thinking. With an inwardness of heart that is felt all the more deeply, they will give to the intellectual person the love that person is lacking.

To the person who always only thinks and thinks and then thinks some more, for whom interpersonal relationships are a rather cool affair because he does not really know what to do with his heart, the people he meets may say: 'What good does your proud intellect really do you? What use is always being right if you can neither give nor receive love? Good luck with your infallible logic; I for one can't make anything of it and would rather look for other people!' A person who flaunts their cleverness and even imagines they are never wrong, will eventually become unbearable to those around them, and will even drive their best friends away. One-sided emphasis on reason is a sign that a person has not yet fully gauged the importance of heart-forces. A head-person finds it hard to understand that there are things in life that only the heart understands.

In modern society—which has devoted itself one-sidedly to the iron logic of science and technology, where feelings and warmth of heart only get in the way of the cult practised by the brain—there are more and more people who are not even aware that there is such a thing as a 'logic of the heart'. They suffer terribly when their business ventures fail, when they experience setbacks in the world of work, they don't care about their heart which could tell them an infinite amount about their life, but which can't even experience setbacks because it has already stopped beating.

The inner mobility arising from the opposite tendencies of head and heart can give every action a person performs the healthy impetus that advances them along their life's path. The intellect has the tendency to focus chiefly on personal advantage, and the heart has the ability to consider what is important to others as well. With our intellect we carefully calculate what we need; in our hearts we can have a feeling for the needs of others. In every situation in life, happiness consists in both thinking of ourselves and in being able to feel with others.

The more rational the profession a person pursues, the more they are required to exclude their heart from the world of work and to let only the cold logic of expediency and utilitarian thinking prevail. The same person will consciously or unconsciously look all the more for a balancing out of this at home, they will then perhaps expect from the people in their immediate environment, from their family, all the feelings and loving attention they are denied in their professional life. They will take the view that at least at home they have the right to 'recharge' a bit. It doesn't occur to them that you can only heed the heart if it has not already been frozen beforehand at the office.

## From heart without head to head without heart

Like everything else in the human being, the interplay between head and heart, between intellect and love, is constantly evolving. In this we can distinguish three consecutive stages: heart without head, head versus heart, and head and heart together.

The first is the stage of nature-given love, where the heart seeks to love without the head, so to speak. Here human beings experience a kind of natural predominance of the heart. Only with the awakening of independent thinking can they take their life into their own hands. Until then they are led by the forces of nature to which the heart also belongs with its yearnings and ideals. The first stage of the head-heart relationship is a form of childhood, a stage in which feelings are not yet illumined by rational thinking or the intellect.

This has been evident in the development of humanity as a whole. If we go back in history only five or six centuries to the time before the emergence of modern science, we find that the forces of the heart and of faith still played a far more significant role in all areas of life than any rational knowledge. In the natural love of a mother for her new-born child, self-love and love of the other are not yet properly separated, especially since the child is not yet an independent being. On the one hand, what also applies in this case is that:

*love without rational mind is self-love.*

On the other hand, natural self-love can embrace many other people apart from one's own self. Only the awakening of the intellect contracts natural self-love in such a way that it begins to concern itself primarily with its own person. Other people, even family members, then recede into the background, a feeling of alienation develops and the natural human connections that were previously experienced as a given, are lost. They must be subsequently re-established in a new way. This requires a new kind of expansion of self-love—this time, however, by free choice—which becomes a difficult but also a gratifying developmental task.

The forces of logical thinking come to maturity in the adult and join the forces of feeling. Every adult then has both heart and mind powers, but life looks very different depending on whether the head or the heart takes the lead. When a person begins to experience the power of reason in adolescence, they will tend at first to pay little attention to the voice of the heart. A person who is completely dependent on the coolly calculating intellect, if not for self-realization then at least for self-preservation and self-assertion, will hardly find enough time and energy to pay full attention to the world of feelings as well.

Thus the second stage in the relationship between love and intellect is where logical thinking takes the lead. Just as people experience their puberty as a separation from their fellow human beings, so the head experiences its own puberty at this second stage as a separation from the heart. Rational thinking, the intellect, is in a certain respect comparable to self-love: initially self-love cannot find the right balance towards love of the other, it must first develop one-sidedly because every individual must first become something themself before they can be something for others. It is no different with the forces of logical thinking: the human being can initially only develop these in a certain opposition to the gifts of nature, and above all to natural love.

Thus many intellectually-oriented people look down on heart-oriented individuals because these intellectuals think that love, in order to become a full expression of a more mature human freedom, must learn to be guided by thought, by the objectivity of knowledge. At this second stage, natural development causes people to favour the head at the expense of the heart. And it is precisely this new one-sidedness given to us by nature that gives our freedom the task of reconciling the head with the heart.

While it is relatively easy for a head-person to see through the inadequacies of the innate heart forces, it is difficult for them to recognize their own one-sidedness. A head that cannot appreciate the heart is only half a head, just as love without reason is only the beginning of love. Only an immature intellect can underestimate or even disregard love. Mature thinking, on the other hand, will willingly serve love. Love that still lacks the wisdom of self-aware thinking is a child of nature; intellect which lacks the warmth of love is still an aspect of humanity's emotional puberty. Maturity of the human spirit is characterized by its unceasing striving for an understanding that makes love more and more conscious, ever warmer and freer, and by an unquenchable desire for a love which, only as a love of thinking, can grow constantly in wisdom and insight.

The more important the achievements of science and technology became in the overall development of humanity, and the more the cool rational mind pushed itself into the foreground, the more the head-heart relationship of earlier times became reversed. The person who strives for science, who devotes all their powers to the technical mastery of nature, will tend all too easily to suppress the forces of the heart, to underestimate the importance of love, if not fail to recognize it altogether.

There is no question that modern science is oriented very much towards the head and very little towards the heart. Love plays no part in it. Many scientists still insist that ethics have nothing to do with their research. They proceed as though their research could only serve an objective knowledge of nature and the progress of humanity. Knowledge as such is always to be welcomed; it is beneficial for humanity under all circumstances because more knowledge means more and more freedom. However, many scientists either do not see or do not want to see how deeply today's research is influenced in its methods and results by the researcher's personal objectives. In their striving for knowledge, people come to completely different results depending on whether they have economic advantage in mind or whether they are guided by a genuine love for nature and humankind.

Just imagine what would happen in a physics, chemistry, or biology laboratory if someone were to start talking there about love in connection with the research. 'What has love got to do with it? How is love involved with what we are doing here?' people would wonder. 'Love is completely out of place here,' they would respond indignantly. And yet, excluding love from any human activity means ignoring the most important thing in life: namely, the question of morality, the question of good and evil. This is actually of the highest importance for us since it is the question of what is genuinely good for humanity, what contributes to its development or hinders it.

The essence of morality is love for humanity, and everything done for the sake of humanity will be morally good. Even nature is like a crystallized morality, because the purpose in all its forces and rhythms of life is to provide humanity with the foundation it needs for its evolution. But questions of morality or ethics are precisely what science and technology are reluctant to concern themselves with, if at all. For modern science, the following applies:

*The rational mind without love can understand everything—*
*except the human being.*

Research today attaches the greatest importance to the progress of technology, to new discoveries and inventions that are intended to increase people's physical well-being. Science and business deal almost exclusively with things having to do with material existence. In Western culture people's thinking, their intellect, has been dedicated to serving and satisfying all the needs of the body. To be sure, this way of thinking has been more inventive in projects of warfare than in projects of charity. But this literally means turning the human being upside down, because humanity can only become happy by putting all the machines in the world at the service of humankind, when the role played by these machines is solely a helping one on the path towards peace and a love that encompasses all of humanity and not the opposite.

'Make love, not war' was the slogan of many protest demonstrations by young people. Of course this is sooner said than done in a world where the education of young people teaches them all about power and warfare—starting with the ruthless competition in economics—and almost nothing about the art of love. Thus we see a new generation of female soldiers, footballers, and even female boxers emerging in the competition of the sexes. Such 'professions' have to be exercised nowadays with such a degree of aggressiveness that one can ask oneself whether people still have a right to complain that there is so little love in the world.

Modern science regards nature as a world available to man solely for productive purposes, there to be exploited by anyone for anything. Many have the idea that humanity's power over nature is unlimited and should not be restricted. Even abuse of animals is often perpetrated for selfish human purposes. This science has produced a society that is fully committed to materialist values. The entire Western world would come to a standstill, even collapse, if it suddenly had no electricity for a month, for example. What is important for this kind of science, this modern technology, is to be constantly extending the scope of 'what is feasible' to infinity, which means inventing new machines, engaging in more and more 'production', producing more and more goods of all kinds.

In this way, however, humanity becomes increasingly dependent on its own products, on devices of all kinds, and the existing imperatives of nature, which it actually wants to overcome, are only extended by further material constraints. For science and technology, religion and morality are something that ought to remain a purely private affair, something which the individual should deal with on their own in their own private sphere. Religion may deal with things like feeling, ethics and morality, but it should do so only as a side-line in life. In public life, morality is only a disruptive factor that impedes 'progress'. Entanglement in the world of machines, and a feeling of tedium towards other people, are mutually reinforcing factors since all too often a passion for technology extinguishes love for people.

When head and heart, intellect and love, machine and man, are experienced as two separate worlds, when human beings lead two separate lives, this is the optimal situation to cause a split in people and hollow them out. Human beings can only experience inner fulfilment when head and heart enliven each other once more, when intellect and feeling support each other, because they are created for one another. This will not succeed for as long as a public and a private life run separately in parallel to each other, without finding their inner connection.

Fortunately for all people, a century ago in the West a whole new kind of science was introduced by the life's work of Rudolf Steiner. It is a science in which, in all areas of life, head and heart come together. This 'spiritual science' strives for an objective knowledge not only of the visible but also of the invisible world. The proper study of the activity of spirit everywhere in matter gives us the opportunity to love the world and human beings ever more intimately in their mutual relationship. Above all, Christianity, the religion of the Being and working of Love, is made the subject of scientific research. Only deepened knowledge can make faith unshakable, and love, in its striving for deeper knowledge, can only ever become more devout. Faith without knowledge of the spiritual is no longer enough for many Christians today. The forces of thought have been directed almost exclusively hitherto to the conquest of the outside world, but people want to be able to engage these forces in the field of religion as well, in order to open up a hopeful future for the world.

This brings us to the third possibility in the head-heart relationship, which consists of a harmony between the two. Here human beings begin to love thinking in their heart, and to seek a science of love with their head. The heart falls in love with the head and the head recognizes the wisdom of the heart. Love learns to love thinking; and reason, through love, becomes not only knowing but also wise. At this third stage of development the individual no longer feels like half a human being who has to decide for just the head *or* just the heart, but like a full human being who experiences head *and* heart as inseparable from each other.

When thinking begins to enlighten love, and when love begins to permeate thinking with warmth, thinking becomes a deeper religion of the heart and love becomes a new art of science. At the third stage of the head-heart relationship,

*rational love*
*and loving reason*
*are the happiness of the human being.*

Every person has their own 'alchemy' of light and warmth, of insight and love. What is particularly beautiful in a person is the unique way in which truth and beauty come to expression in them. In order truly to love someone, we must get to know them in their uniqueness, and the better we know someone the more reasons we find to love them from the heart. For, being human means not only having the capacity for unlimited love but also of being worthy of it. For all of nature it is only too 'natural' to love humanity. For people it is not entirely natural to love their fellow human beings because their love can be more than simply natural: it can only be achieved in freedom and it ought to be given completely freely. Nature gives human beings a longing for a love that they must first attain out of their freedom.

Striving for knowledge gives love the strength, in our association with others, to do not only what is good for oneself, but above all what is good for the other. A person's knowledge becomes the deepest desire of love, for only through love can the lover know what the other needs and what truly advances them. When what I do for others is something that makes *me* happy, that gives *me* the feeling of being a loving person, I am then simply loving my own need to be loving. In that case I simply like myself in my capacity as a person who loves. There is nothing wrong with this self-love as long as it is not confused with love for others. If, on the other hand, I make an effort to see objectively what the other person really needs at this moment, and if I then act on this regardless of whether it gives me pleasure or not, then I really love them. True love always seeks the light of knowledge.

If someone tells me they feel understood by me, this has far greater moral weight than if they tell me they are happy because I like them. It is easy to love others if at this moment we feel like it—anyone can do that. The effort of learning better and better to know another person and their path, of knowing and doing what they need in order to help them move forward, requires a much stronger power of love than just liking them. Thinking is the organ of knowledge, and only love of thinking can give us the strength to put aside all the things that please or displease us in order really to support and encourage the other in their unique character.

In the last few centuries humanity has put all the power of its thinking at the service of science. The time has now come to put it at the service of a science of the human being. It is now a matter of finding the courage to dedicate the same selfless objectivity with which people have pursued their scientific research of the external world, to a knowledge of the human being. Every individual only really knows what they love, because love must always be preceded by deeper understanding.

Nature does not only give us our first love (self-love) which does not yet know love of the other, but also our first knowledge (knowledge of nature) which does not yet know the human being because it cannot evaluate the moral weight of love. In both cases, what is best in life is left to human freedom: the happiness, when we attain our second love (love for each person), of transforming our first love into something wholesome. And it is left to our freedom, through love for the second knowledge (knowledge of the human being) also to give back to natural science its true meaning. Thus love and knowledge never wish to cease looking for, and mutually supporting, each other. In human beings and through human beings they are constantly striving towards each other, for the heart lives in its longing for the advice of the head, and the intellect longs for the promptings of love.

# Justice is calculating, love is lavish

The relationship between love and justice is similar to that between love and reason. In order to be just, justice also requires a rational assessment of things. Every right decision, every fair approach can only be made by way of an objectively weighed logic.

What is the relationship between justice and love? This is an essential question, because how people live together socially depends on its answer. Western culture, in so far as it would like to call itself Christian, is founded on the conviction that two thousand years ago the most significant turn in all our development was ushered in. Prior to this turn, the decisive factor was justice; since the turn, it is love that is to take on the leading role more and more. In Mosaic Law, in the Jewish Torah, the main emphasis was placed on the Ten Commandments, where the good man was the righteous one, the *tsadik*. In the spirit of the Christian Gospels, the good man is the one who is permeated by the essence of love. The meaning of evolution, seen in a Christian light, lies in the fact that love for justice seeks to transform itself more and more into a justice of love. This change can only take place in the heart of each individual.

Many might object here that if people were really 'righteous' among themselves, if they were able to treat each other fairly, that would surely be more than enough, everything would be fine. What more would we need if everyone was given exactly what they were entitled and had a right to?

The fundamental principle of justice is that all people are equal. If all people were to be treated according to this principle, they would all have to be granted the same. If you gave more to one person and less to another, or something completely different to one than to another, you would be acting unjustly. If all people are equal, no one has the right to be 'more equal' than anyone else.

And yet equality, when applied one-sidedly, can become the most unjust thing in the world. This is so because as true as it is that all people are equal, it is equally true that no one is the same as anyone else. All people are equally dissimilar, each person is completely different. Everyone is the same with respect to their common human dignity in so far as no human being can be more or less of a human being than any other. But all the things that make this common humanity concrete and individual—our abilities, plans, activities, ideals, circumstances, to cite just the most obvious—are different from one person to the next. What is helpful for one person might not be good in the same way for another. In order to 'do justice' to the specific needs of each person in the same way, one would have to treat each individual in a completely different and quite 'unequal' way. How is it possible to reconcile justice, which would like to see everyone treated equally, with the different treatment due to each individual in recognition of their particular nature?

The pursuit of justice is expressed in the social contract of a society's laws, which is why they are equally valid for all. They are indispensable for societal life because they create the necessary framework on which all individuals depend in the same way for their ability to act. But for one striving for freedom, the things required of us comprise the foundation of freedom, everything we have in common is only the indispensable prerequisite for what is individual.

Just as knowledge is the necessary prerequisite for a deepened love, but remains deficient and one-sided if it does not serve love, so the law that strives for justice is also the necessary basis for loving solidarity, but it is no less one-sided and deficient if it fails to serve love in the context of society.

Thus it is impossible for the justice of love to treat all people the same because each person is completely different from every other. Justice is merely concerned with people in general, whereas love is always concerned with *this* individual in particular. Love presupposes the things that are just and necessary for all, and adds to them the thousand ideas of its moral fantasy, which are beneficial in the individual case. Justice gives everyone what is necessary and the same for everyone. Mere justice is unable to do justice to the individual person in their distinct uniqueness—only love can do this. Love gives much more than merely what is necessary; it gives each one something different, and gives it completely differently in each case.

Justice deals with the common good; only love can take care of the happiness of the individual. The cool intellect is right in wanting to treat everybody equally justly, but love claims the higher right of doing right by the uniqueness of each individual as well. Just laws that apply equally to everyone are less and less adequate in times of increasing individualization, in times when every individual wants to live out their own distinct uniqueness.

A society that only recognizes laws that are universally applicable will suppress the particularity of the individual. If the law prevents what is individual, it becomes 'unjust' to all because it does not take into account every person's uniqueness and thus does everyone wrong to the highest degree. The art of the life of society lies in aspiring to the proper balance between justice and love. Everything to do with legality can be managed centrally and uniformly, it can be looked after by the state because it has general validity, because it is intended to be enforced uniformly everywhere. With the very individual talents and needs of each individual, however, it is exactly the opposite: these can only be taken into account 'locally' in the personal encounter between one person and another. Striving for justice is the task of the community; cultivating love is the vocation of the individual. If one insists on the equality of people and neglects love, this leads to levelling down and ultimately to indifference, to the social coldness that can be experienced everywhere today. If, in the name of an abstract equality, we always have only the generality in mind without looking at what is specific to the individual, people become hollow inside, they become just part of a template like sheep in a flock or soldiers in an army. And many individuals will rebel against this—all the more so if they fail to see that the problem is not so much the presence of what makes us all equal, but rather the absence, the lack, of what individualizes us. The maturity and well-being of a society depend entirely on the number of individuals who do not expect from the administration of justice, from an all-equalizing state, that which only love for the individual human being—which is usually somewhat shyly called 'solidarity'—can do and actually does do.

What does a nurse get out of observing all the rules that apply equally to everyone working in her field? Will she experience inner fulfilment if she *only* follows the external regulations? What good does it do a teacher if he or she merely obeys instructions and sticks to the curriculum? Is it enough for a judge to know every paragraph of the law by heart to do justice to this 'individual case', this particular person on whom he has to pass judgement? A nurse will only find inner fulfilment in her work when she treats the patients in need of her care in a completely different way from all other nurses in the world. 'What' she is in terms of her profession, is something she has in common with millions of others, but her particular 'how' depends entirely on her creative capacity, on her love.

How she treats patients, what she experiences as she does so, and what the patients experience through her, is a 'world' that exists nowhere else except where she is. Many women have motherhood in common. But no mother, in how she treats her child, wants to have to follow the usual universal rules. She wants to be a mother in a completely different way from every other mother, and in a different way also for each of her children.

Justice has to do with rights and responsibilities. A just law prescribes what everyone ought to do or not do, quite irrespective of whether they want to or not. In relation to the law, people can only experience a negative freedom: they can willingly do what they are legally obliged to do, or voluntarily refrain from doing what is prohibited. Love on the other hand, is a kind of higher justice that presupposes and includes in itself everything that is just. It acts beyond any prescriptions or prohibitions. What is prescribed by law has nothing to do with freedom, and what love does has only to do with freedom. Love also does what we are obliged to do, but of its own free will; it respects a just law voluntarily, because it does so for the sake of everyone's freedom. But it does much more of 'the good' than is required by law and avoids much more of 'the bad' than is forbidden by law. Love is boundless generosity, love is superabundance. Justice gives in measured portions, love gives in excess because it insists on being lavish.

The law that applies to everyone is like the soil in a garden. It is the same for all the plants and flowers, and they all need it. But in the same soil and under the same climatic conditions, a thousand different flowers can bloom. Even when the sunshine, water, and air are the same for all, the flowers growing there are never all the same, indeed no two will ever be exactly the same in form and colour. But this is precisely what is beautiful in the life of society! The purpose of societal coexistence is not the observance of laws that are just for everyone, but rather the creation of the fertile soil that each person needs in order to 'invent' their own personal, individual life. Just laws are like the monochrome light of society; love for the individual generates from that light the thousand varied colours that make life worth living. It goes without saying that it is easier to be just than to do love justice. But here the adage applies that 'easier' does not always mean 'better'. In this case it is precisely what is difficult that is better, because nothing can be better for the human being than love.

# Justice can exist without love, but not love without justice

A strong impression we gain from an unbiased observation of today's world is that people are actually in the midst of a great turning-point in their development. Fewer and fewer people are satisfied with what is considered just, and those who regard the edicts of justice as unjust are growing more numerous. And it is no longer enough for us to do only what we are all *supposed* or *obliged* to do. Everyone is looking for the space to do what they do, because this is what they *wish for* out of their innermost freedom. Everyone would like to find a way to realize themself, a way that is 'right' for them only and for no one else, because only they can 'do justice' to their special nature. Only on such a special path can full justice be done to each individual person.

We need only look at very everyday interpersonal relationships: when two people live together, it is inevitable that they will argue again and again about what is considered just or unjust. 'I have a right to it... you're being unfair!' 'No, you're the one being unfair! I have rights too.' This can often go back and forth for hours on end. And if both individuals stick to what they consider everyone thinks is just or unjust, they will never come to agreement. It repeatedly happens that one person demands something from the other which they consider to be their right, and the other feels this to be completely unjustified. How often do we hear the sentence: 'No, you're asking too much!'

Why does what the other asks of me always seem too much to me? It is because what they want from me basically has no limit: they want everything from me and are never satisfied. But the strange thing is that I demand no less from them, I also have just as much of an impression that what they give me is always too little. I also feel it is only fair if they never rebut me or say no, and maybe even then it is not enough for me!

This is just one of many signs that the great turning-point that began for Christianity two thousand years ago is still in full swing today. The intellect, which coolly weighs up the justice of a matter, is waiting in all spheres of life to make way gradually to a generosity of heart that seeks to be more than merely legal. People have never sought love with a deeper longing than they do today, because love alone can give each of us infinitely more than what is merely legal.

At this point, someone might argue that reasonable justice also knows how to take account of the heart. But how does the intellect think or make its calculations? It looks at life externally and thinks, 'When I was little my parents took care of me and gave me food and clothing. Later they provided the necessary funds for my education, and then they helped me find a job. When I got married, they bought me a fridge and a washing machine, and yesterday they gave me a bottle of wine. Well, tomorrow I can give them something in return for the bottle of wine. But we can take it as a given that they would raise me and then support me for a while. That's the right thing to do; that's how everyone does it. Did I ask them to bring me into the world? And after all, when I have children, it will be the same for me as it was for them. In the end, it all balances out…'

Love's 'bill', on the other hand, looks very different. A truly loving person says to themselves: 'I have not only received from others everything I *have*, but on top of that I also owe them for everything I *am*! So what should I be giving back? What do I rightfully owe others? I owe them my whole being, my whole existence! Quite simply: *everything*.'

The kind of justice that only love is capable of is based on the conviction that each of us owes everything to everyone else, and the heart feels just only when it passes on everything it has received: its abilities, its strengths, its time—in short, everything, without offsetting the one against the other. If it holds back even the slightest thing, it immediately feels this to be unfair. The only righteousness love knows lies in its desire to give itself unconditionally.

We human beings are basically all good little egotists who demand a kind of justice that has to look absolutely reasonable. Just think of the struggle raging today against international terrorism and ask yourself who is right and who is wrong in this fight. Imagine the President of the United States making the following speech to his people about the state of the nation: 'My fellow Americans, I urge you to love all the terrorists in the world! We stand in their debt, for we have only been able to create the prosperity we enjoy by unjustly exploiting all of humanity and the environment. We ourselves have turned these people into so-called terrorists by our own injustice. It is only fair that we now give back everything we have taken from them. We have no right to attack any country with the excuse of preventing terrorism. If we do this, we are only enforcing the law of "might is right". But it was precisely in the struggle against the "right" of a mightier nation, of England at that time, that our nation was born.' If he spoke like this, how would his voters respond? They would probably all cry out, 'He's lost his mind! We need new elections. We must have a new president.'

For a century mankind has been as though obsessed with a motto that attaches the utmost importance to justice between nations. It says: 'All peoples have an equal right to self-determination.' What could sound more obvious than this truism? And yet, what is the reality? Just think of relations between the Palestinians and Israelis in the Middle East, between Protestants and Catholics in Northern Ireland, between the peoples of the Balkans, between Muslims, Christians and Hindus in the Far East. What does it mean in such cases to say 'All peoples have an equal right to self-determination'? How just is the justice that each side claims for itself? This slogan about the right of all nations to self-determination threatens to throw humanity back to the mentality that prevailed, and rightly so at that time, before the above-mentioned turning-point two thousand years ago. At that time justice sufficed because the striving for freedom had not yet awakened in the individual human being. In our time, this slogan is a tragic anachronism, something completely out of date, because an equalizing justice, without love for the uniqueness of each individual, can no longer be just. How would things look in a family where each family member's right to self-determination was the only thing that counted, and there was no mutual love?

In a lecture given on 20 December 1918, Rudolf Steiner describes a gigantic spiritual battle currently taking place in the spiritual world between wisdom and love. Spiritual beings, full of wisdom, had previously seen to it that everything found its rightful place. They had created a wise, rational and just order in the world. But now the spirits of love are beginning to lead development—and this brings many things into confusion. Wisdom loves the old traditional order, but love invents something new every day. The order of wisdom sees good in the beauty of the world; the order of love looks for beauty in the goodness of people. Those who want wisdom without love want peace and quiet, but this peace and quiet is like a graveyard. Things in a graveyard may look nice and orderly, but it is still there, nothing stirs. Those who try to unite wisdom with love are pursuing a higher order, a world full of surprises in which every person can develop completely freely in their own uniqueness.

Those who only want order are afraid of love, but it is not nice to live in fear of love. Order is indeed necessary, but what use is order without love? The human being was not created for order, but all order for the human being. Love is creative, is able to create a new order every day, because the only order it knows is the kind that is always changing. This requires a higher degree of moral imagination, but precisely this is what actually corresponds to a world where everything is in a state of becoming, where all people are on their way together.

Loving every person every day in a different way means wanting more than just order. Justice would like to preserve the old traditional order which it sees as justified because it has been proven to 'function'. Love, on the other hand, invents life anew every day because it is inexhaustibly creative. If everything is done according to order but with an absence of love, then we still have the absence of everything that can make people happy.


## Aware of the past, loving the future

The experience of time is of great significance for people. Memories of the past, of our experiences, the plans for the future that a person strives towards, meet in our present. At every moment we experience in our mind something like an equilibrium that arises from the balance between our past and our future. Here again the forces of the intellect and of love serve again and again to find a proper balance. The past becomes a matter of knowledge in so far as it can be perceived objectively; in other words, intellect and reason grasp the things of their own past with the same factual sobriety with which the objectivity of natural laws is explored.

The opposite is the case for the future. There nothing objective is to be seen as yet; there we turn to the power of love because love can deal with the future better than reason can. For, love means trusting in the future development of capacities that are already present, even before we know with any precision what the individual in their freedom will do with them. A loving person looks at their loved one with a heart full of confidence, full of hope and faith in their talents. Love means always joyfully taking the risk of the other's freedom. Love for their future is love for their freedom. In order to love this freedom, love must be happy to take risks, and in order to love the risk, it must have nothing to lose.

A mother loves her child because its future is more important by far than its past. Her hope, the strong faith of her love, can imagine a future full of promise. It must have been like this for the Godhead with regard to humanity, since being human can be seen as the childhood stage of being a god. In the eyes of their creator, human beings must have far more future ahead of them than past behind them. The Godhead must have created human beings with the love of a mother, it must love their hopeful future, their becoming-divine, above all else. The world really looks as though divine love took the great evolutionary risk of human freedom with full determination. The world looks as though it was created for the sake of all people in order to offer every human being the most hopeful future.

Every person has a head to recognize better and better what was brought about by the past. The heart, on the other hand, love, is given to us in order constantly to produce new creations for the future. Love has a feeling, a sense, for what one individual or another can become, it has the gift of presentiment, something the intellect has no notion of.

Love decides the future because intellectual knowledge has nothing to say about it. When the status quo makes the decisions about how things are to proceed, it only results in a repetition of the same, similar to the laws of nature. If things stay as they were, then there is an absence of love whose talent lies in creating only what is new. And if evolution is realized only through the creative production of the new, then it is impossible for man to have arisen from the apes because, in order to produce man, the ape would already have to bear man in itself as a pre-disposition, as the child bears the adult. But in that case the ape would be a nascent man and not an ape. And just as every child turns into an adult human being, so every ape would have to turn into an adult human being, which is clearly not the case.

The human being can only have arisen in the imagination of the creative love of spiritual beings who wanted to create, apart from the apes, something completely different, a creature in their own image, endowed with reason and love. And this is precisely what love is: the power constantly to invent something new, to constantly bring forth 'creation out of nothing'. For love, what already exists is a foundation, a necessary starting-point, a tool for the new that is to be created, but never its deciding cause. Love never needs an already-existing model to copy because it never repeats the same things. Love is the art of saying 'I love you' a thousand times without repeating yourself.

Another important polarity of living in time is the contrast between power and love. The management of what already exists requires the exercise of power. But the constraints on this management repeatedly tempt power to use people as a tool to maintain the status quo. Thus it is the task of love again and again to neutralize the inhumanity of power. Love is the art of using everything as a tool *for* humanity, and never as the art of using people *as* a tool for other purposes.

Power wants to monitor everything; love has no need to monitor because it has full trust in everyone. Those who want power don't like taking risks that could jeopardize their power; those who love have the strength to endure every abyss of freedom, because for them the freedom of the loved one is their greatest good. A person who has power can force others, if those others are dependent on that power, to do certain things. The happiness of love consists in not having to force anyone to do anything, and being able not to be forced by anyone. The relationship between freedom and love results in something like a formula of happiness that looks like the following deduction:

> *Only freedom*
> *makes people happy;*
> *people are free only in love;*
> *therefore only love*
> *makes people happy.*

Because love does not rely on power, because it rejects power of any kind, it can never be made dependent on power. It cannot be blackmailed in any way because it has nothing to lose. This explains why someone who truly loves can also be strict and implacable when this is what love demands. When it is a matter of the loved one's well-being, love has the strength to be uncompromising. This is exactly how a mother deals with her small child: she can be utterly unyielding when it comes to her child's well-being. People might not always like what is done to them out of love, but it is always for their own good.

Another mysterious quality of love is its complete 'infallibility'. A loving heart not only has a sense for what the future will bring, it also follows with heartfelt interest every step in the loved one's development. The infallibility of love lies in its mobility: it is so inventive, so versatile, that in any situation in life it is always able to find exactly what's needed. Love is not infallible because what it does *is* always right, but because things are *made right* through love. The intellect may say *what* should be done, but love is the art of the *how*. And in most things in life, particularly where people are concerned, the *how* is far more important than the *what*. Where there is love, every act is right—and this through the love itself since only love is always right. Where love is absent every decision is wrong, every partner is the wrong one because one is oneself the wrong partner through one's own lovelessness. Everything we do without love will not last. Where there is love, everything the human being does will turn out for the good.

Two people who love one another are always right for each other because love makes each the right one in a new way every day. Two people will always be wrong for each other when love is absent. It is not the other's love for *me* that makes them the right one for me, but only my love for *them*. It is never the person not loved by others who is lonely, but rather the person who does not love. One who loves will never feel lonely, least of all when they are alone, because their heart is always brimming over with the people they love.

## Islamic science in Western culture

In order to better understand the relationship between love and reason, it can be helpful to look at the current dispute between Islam and Christianity. A key point of this debate is the fact that in Christianity the Son of God who became man is no less important than the Father God. In the Gospels, this son prefers to call himself the 'son of man'. This means that if God became man, then this man can, in his own way, become 'God'. This gradual development towards the divine is to be made possible for all human beings precisely through God's becoming human himself. The essence of Christianity is the inexhaustible love of the divine Son for every human being, a love that makes possible a limitless evolution for everyone. Christianity is love for the individual freedom and developmental potential of every human being, because the Son of God gives every human being the capacity for a divine love.

The Koran starts from a completely different premise: at the centre of Islam is Almighty God, the unlimited omnipotence of Allah. An important repeated statement in the Koran is that Allah is the only God, and he has no son. Thus Islam does not recognize a divine Son of man, and, as a result of this fact, the free creation of the individual human being, the individualized human spirit, plays hardly any role in Islam at all.

In the Christian trinity, the meaning of the Son-become-man lies in the fact that providence is made in the divine plan for God willingly to renounce His continued omnipotence in the inner human being. This divine renunciation leaves room for human freedom. God the Father does not only love Himself in the human being, but loves far more the divine Son of man in every human being. In His Son He renounces His omnipotence so that the Son may ignite the power of love in the human heart. The Son of God is thus every human being in their freedom and uniqueness, and the whole of humanity in its oneness and diversity.

Human beings, in the Christian sense, follow the experience of the divine Son when they become ever more free, ever more creative in their thinking, ever more loving and responsible in their actions. The Son whom Christians call 'Christ', does not wish to work omnipotently in human beings because then they could not be free—and without freedom they cannot love. The Christ works with love, and this means that what is close to his heart above all is to make each individual human being ever more capable of freedom, ever more creative. Loving always means wishing for the freedom of the beloved. The essence of Christianity is the love with which Christ loves humanity: a love that is so great, so boundless, that to the clever people of this world it seems utterly foolish. A love that forgoes the exercise of any power—for the sake of human freedom. 'How absurd! You have done so much for others and healed so many, so now show us what you can do for yourself! Come down from the cross, show us your power if you really think you are the son of the Almighty.' These, in essence, are the words that are recorded of those who stood under the cross. . . .

We might ask ourselves what if anything has remained of this spirit of Christ after two thousand years. It is not the power of a Church that can keep this spirit of love alive but always only the human individual striving for inner freedom and love. If Christianity is the science of love, then every individual who understands love and for whom love is the most important thing in life, is a Christian. Nothing is more important to one who loves than the inner freedom of the loved one. If divine love gives every person the faculty of freedom, it is the task of the human being to exercise this faculty, to foster it in every individual.

Because the aspiration of Christianity is the highest there is—the aspiration of love—there is in Christian culture, perhaps more than in any other, a yawning gap between theory and reality. The reality that has emerged in Christian countries in the last two thousand years looks far more like the spirit of Islam than the true spirit of Christianity. The Christian religion has had far less influence on culture in the West than our thoroughly Islamic natural science whose basic principle is exactly the same as that of the Koran. This principle states that the human being is pervasively determined by natural laws, and so-called freedom is merely an illusion, a vain self-deception. Fundamentally speaking, the same thing is said by Islam when it claims that only Almighty Allah determines human beings. Whether what imperatively determines humanity is traced back to the laws of nature or to the will of God or Allah, this does not change the fact that the human being is considered unfree in both cases, and this is what is decisive in both Western science and culture, and Islam, with regard to the human experience of self.

## What happened to Christian love?

Christian religion, the religion of love, today seems enfeebled and lacking in energy. It appears as though leading a meagre existence in the shadow of its church towers. Far from any claims to being scientific, people ponder a faith which, in its indefinite yearning for something long gone, can neither properly live nor die. More and more people feel an emptiness in their hearts because religion has shunned the light of knowledge for too long. The world of work, for its part, is dominated by a dry, heartless science, by an almost brutal technology that threatens to deprive humanity of all freedom.

So what must the great step forward look like? This step can no longer be expected from the power of any group, whether it be the state, the Church, or society. A group is responsible for its power, not for love. It is the same for the power of any institution as it is for justice: it finds its justification to the extent that it creates the necessary foundation for love and serves love—but only the individual human being is capable of loving. Just as justice has to prepare the ground for love, so the group has to prepare the ground for individuality. The moral justification of an establishment lies solely in the love of those within it towards every person. Every enterprise, every organized group of people, is a means to an end: the end must always be the human being, and the individual human being should never be made into a means. In an age when people were still childlike, the Church and state had to take on the role of parents even for the adults. In the present age of individual freedom, claims to leadership by a group are always anachronistic. Today the hour of the individual has struck, humanity as a whole has come of age, and every adult experiences the joys and pains of their puberty on the path to freedom, the phase of their childhood comes to an end.

It is the task of the individual to carry out ever more decisively this change towards individual freedom which has been calling for the logic of the heart now for two thousand years. Every individual is capable of no longer being led in their development by a cold calculating righteousness, or by a science that makes us unfree, but rather by love and freedom, by trust in the creative power of every human spirit. Only the individual human being is able through their love to humanize science, and thus also to liberate love by illuminating it by their thinking. Through the light of knowledge we imbue our love with truth, and, through the power of our love, we redeem science of its un-human quality. Love is freed from the instincts of egotism whenever we understand our fellow human beings better. Cold reason is always permeated with warmth when we take the science of love to heart.

'That's all well and good,' some might object, 'but how is this to be done? Where on earth do we start?' If a person doesn't know what to do, it is because they imagine the beginning is somewhere far away outside themself. But the proper beginning can only be when the individual sees that 'I can only begin with myself, it is exclusively up to me!' We all have a head at our disposal that thinks, and a heart that can give and receive love. The big step forward for me can only be that I resolve to bring more and more thinking, ever more objective knowledge into my misunderstood religion, and ever more freedom and love into my inhuman science. Head and heart can only be brought together in myself, I alone can overcome in myself headless religion and heartless science.

Without laws, people are unsocial, but laws only tame them. Only love makes them free. Our fallen intellect has produced a science without love, and our fallen love, a self-love without love for others. The coldness of the intellect and the constraint of self-love, which all people must experience daily at close quarters, create in them the longing, on the path of inner change, to give warmth to their head and light to their heart. The great change in all development is carried out by each of us in our day-to-day lives, with every step, no matter how small, towards greater freedom and love.

# 5. Love and Life

*The Social Art in the Age of Freedom*

## Realism and Idealism: the created world and the world still to be created

With our rational mind we can stand with both feet firmly on the ground in the midst of the visible world. The heart forces of our love can give us wings to lift ourselves up into the world of the highest ideals. The intellect reckons with the world as it is. Love cannot be satisfied with this; it is constantly seeking a better and more beautiful world—too beautiful, too good to possibly become complete reality, since striving is itself part of love's nature. People are only happy when they are aspiring and creative, like artists who love the creations of their imagination like their own children. Full of hope, they carry their ideas until the hour of their birth into the world.

Only the heart never loses hope in a better future, but without ideals the best forces in the human being desiccate. It is the task of the intellect to take account of the past, to concern itself with what is already extant, since this is the foundation for all further creativity and idealism. Idealism divorced from reality is vain utopia, selfish over-excited enthusiasm, loveless escapism. On the other hand, sober realism, which is not interested in ideals, produces nothing but inflexible, small-minded buyers and sellers. There is really enough in the world of what today is called 'realism'; what is lacking at every corner is a love for great ideals. This emptiness inside people has made the world a sad and depressing place.

Ideals are the substance out of which love is made. When a person loves them with all their heart, these ideals shape and enliven the world. Initially we can only accept the world as it is, but what an individual wishes to create out of themself must first take shape in their imagination, in the best part of the human being. Every ideal was once a thought, an idea that occurred to a creative imagination.

Everyday life puts the breaks on idealism in everyone, obstructs it with a thousand obstacles. The so-called realist is always eager to point out that one cannot change much in the existing world anyway, so why bother? He looks at the thousand things around him over which he has no influence and compared to which the few possibilities he does have seem futile. He fails to see that what he is doing is like a girlfriend who, when her boyfriend gives her a rose as a token of his love, instead of rejoicing at his love, says, 'What is a single rose compared to the thousands of roses you haven't given me!' Thus for the modern materialist the sense-perceptible world, like the rose for the girlfriend, is no longer a token of its invisible riches—for which he has little understanding—but only the cause of his bemoaned lack of happiness.

Love opens up a completely different kind of account. It does not focus on what it cannot change in the existing world, because for love it is never a matter of changing what already exists but rather of always creating something of its own, bringing something completely new into the world. Only in creating the new does love seek to meet the existing world in order to transform it in such a way that the new enriches it. Those who want only to change what already exists will be determined in their actions by what others have done. Because they produce nothing new or of their own, they gnaw away at the existing world and blame it for their dissatisfaction which in reality is the result of their own lack of creative imagination. They demand that the world provide them with their inner fulfilment, forgetting that all it can provide is the ground for their own free creativity.

A truly innovative love wishes to see the existing world as a tool in the hand of the artist in each of us, who then, in accordance with his creative imagination, freely gives shape to the new. No tool, however, can help those who are not in a position to produce anything out of themselves, the whole world cannot help them, much less their criticism of it. An artist with a rich imagination is never occupied with painting over pictures that already exist—what he wants is always to create new ones. For the artist it is not a matter of improving the old, but always of creating something better.

Love is the ability to engage and act creatively wherever the possibility arises. And it arises everywhere. One who aspires in a loving way to ideals beneficial to humanity, always finds opportunities for their free deeds. It is not a question of the number of things a person does, but of their creative power itself, for it is this that makes the human being happy. It then seems to people that the whole world was created only to make their own creativity possible. One who can act imaginatively will be so happy, so tirelessly occupied, that they will have no time to get stuck in thinking about what they can't change or what they can't do.

Love only experiences those ideals as giving us wings and joy which have the potential, bit by bit, to become reality. An ideal that could not engage with and intervene in reality in any way would be nothing but a chimera, a castle in the air. If we were to ask an idealist, 'What have you achieved with your nice ideals? Look around, there is not much to see of them!' they could answer: 'All my ideals have always been a powerful reality in me, otherwise I should not have been able to create the thousand things I have achieved up to now. But how do you think the world as it is now came into being? Only by people who once had an idea and decided it was such a good idea that they made it an ideal for everything they aspired to, so that then, in the course of time, they realized this ideal in the visible world.'

This is precisely what the dry rational mind can barely understand, namely that love for ideals is a much stronger, more effective force than all the dry sense of reality in the world, because everything that is visible has arisen from an idea. Short-sighted realism cannot see that people's internal world—their thoughts, goals, aspirations—is far more decisive in the course of the world than all external reality. Idealists have something like an innate sense for this fundamental truth in life. Their intellect may not always be able to explain this logically, but their heart feels it with an unshakable certainty.

When a person has to make a decision, they ask themself, 'What ought I to do, or what do I want to do?' If they look for the answer only in the advice of others, if they allow themselves to be led exclusively by time-worn, traditional, general rules, if they are directed by the existing reality, if they only want to 'play it safe', they extinguish in themselves any hint of ingenuity, of enthusiasm, which would give them the opportunity to set the goals of their actions from their own imagination. The one-sided sobriety of realism arises from an inner insecurity which seeks to feel secure through the support of tangible reality.

The times in which people looked to their pastor, their 'guru' or similar spiritual directors in order to be told from outside how to behave, are gone. The scientifically trained person of today is no longer a child not yet able to find their own path and therefore in need of someone to show them the way. The modern adult, the inwardly independent human being, wants to put their mark on life and the world in an entirely personal way, and this stamp, this unique seal, can only prove to be good because every human being in their innermost being is the creature of a divine love.

Every individual is called upon to be an artist. They have the ability in every situation of life to bring about something uniquely their own. No one needs to be lectured to or admonished from outside if they are genuinely striving to do their best. Every human being has in them enough inventive capacity, talent, and ability to be able to decide for themself how they wish to behave in each encounter. The free human being does willingly what he has to do because he knows that the duty whose fulfilment serves as the basis for the freedom of all, is justified. The person who loves both their own and the other's freedom because they see it as both their highest right and their most sacred duty, is the greatest idealist and realist in one. The inner power that makes us such idealistic and realistic artists is the power of love.


## Love of ideals creates reality

At some point every person is taken up with the question: 'How has the world come about, this world that I can see with my eyes and touch with my hands?' They find the answer when they look at the world produced by man. Here they can also ask, 'How has the world of technology come about with all its machines, how all its discoveries and inventions?' The answer can only be: before all these machines became visible reality, they lived in people as thoughts. Everything people have produced was originally an idea, a thought. An idea that a scientist or researcher produces in their thinking can be so enticing that they literally fall in love with it. They simply can't help but want to realize it. It becomes a powerful ideal in them, it pushes them forward and gives them no rest until it has become a visible fact.

This is how it is wherever there is human activity: a creative idea becomes, through the power of love, an inspiring ideal that strives to manifest, to become external reality. Even the driest realist has to admit that without ideas that have become ideals, I would not have before me anything of what I call reality. Every conjecture, every scientific hypothesis is initially nothing more than an idea, an intuition. In his trials, in his experiments, the scientist's idea becomes an ideal; he wants to bring something about in the objective world that confirms his discovery, something that reveals his discovery in a replicable way for everyone, that makes it visible in other words. This is how the wheel was invented, as well as the clock, the computer, and the aeroplane. It is human thoughts that create the world of technology. Only a humanity devoid of spirit can suppose that the material world is the only real one, and that human ideas are not reality.

A scientist who considers the sense-perceptible world to be the only real world has never thought more deeply about his own activity, has never considered that it is his own activity that gives the lie to his theory. For it is his thoughts that determine how external reality will look—it is created by them. That many researchers are more in love with the idea of some machine than in a person, that they have more love and enthusiasm for an invention than for the people they share their daily life with, only goes to confirm that wherever people strive after goals, *love* is the driving force.

And many a woman would be less opposed to her husband's love affair with his wonderful motor car if only he had some of the same interest and attention left over for her. It is not the love for the machine in itself that she feels to be bad, but the lack of love for human beings. We can already see today how a generation of eleven- and twelve-year-olds barely notice when their uncle or aunt come to visit because they don't want to be distracted from their computer game. As blissful as love for progress in science and technology may be, love for people is a thousand times more blissful—and a thousand times more essential for us! For love of the material world can only really give us joy once it has ceased to be an end in itself and begins to serve love for others.

How much idealism and how much realism is there in the life of the mother of a new-born child? If she looked at it with factual sobriety, what would be so special about the little one who has to be cleaned and changed all the time, who cries and is unable to tell her why, who demands all the mother's time and doesn't even let her sleep at night? This is the sobering reality if we look at the situation completely factually, and in this respect many fathers—without doubt—tend far more towards the realism.

Of course, a mother also feels the burden associated with the care of a small child. But here again her female imagination plays the most important role. Because there is as yet little external reality in the life of her child, the mother leaves debilitating realism to others while she herself dreams up a completely ideal life for her child. Mentally she paints out the most beautiful life for her child since, after all, her child is not just any child but *the* child! A mother's love sees in her child quite simply *the* human being, the ideal human being in all its beauty and perfection.

So what gives a mother the strength to do everything she accomplishes in the absolutely real world, and which many sober rational men would not accomplish? It is the power of love, not just natural love for her child but above all the power of the ideals which bring about far more in reality than the cool intellect alone. How, ultimately, would all the achievements of human thinking and activity have come about if there had been no mother's love to care for and bring up all the scientists and technologists of the world when they were little?

The intellect only understands the world. Love shapes it. And the intellect, to be creative, always needs love. Without the power of love no mother would be able to do what many mothers do. Every mother knows that her child has come into the world in order to realize itself as much as possible as a human being, to experience as much as possible of truth, goodness, and beauty, even to love as much as possible. A mother wishes the best for her child that life can give, all beauty and goodness—not a third of it, not even three quarters of it, but all of it. She knows that as an adult we may say we are lucky if in the end we manage to turn only a fraction of our most beautiful ideals into fact. Naturally she 'knows' this since she also knows the other side of reality. It makes her all the happier that she has a small child here before her, her child, in whom the question as to what kind of person it will be one day is still open, still undecided. For one thing she knows with total certainty is that if the ideals of the future are to be realized, they need the full power of love now.

Maternal love is the embodiment of nature-given love for the human being, is the love for everything good that the human being can become in his or her development. Already by the cradle, a mother sees how her child will one day walk upright, how it will learn to speak and think—three faculties that differentiate the human from the animal and make us a human being. The mother's love for this threefold process of becoming human can later be transformed by the adult individual into consciously and freely developed faculties, and raised to a higher level: to a love of movement, speech, and thinking as creative arts.

Through *natural love* the child learns to walk, speak, and think. In maternal love, *human love*, the unconscious element of nature and the awakened consciousness are in equilibrium. In the adult a fully conscious *love for the human being* can be achieved through individual freedom.

It says in the Gospels: 'Unless you become like the children, you will not be able to enter the kingdom of heaven.' It says, 'unless you *become* like the children,' and not, 'unless you *remain* like the children'. Only an adult can become a child once more by taking up fully consciously and individually what they learnt unconsciously as a child. While thinking is the last faculty the child attains, because walking and speaking are the prerequisite foundation for it, the adult must later begin with thinking since only thinking enables them to attain a new level of thinking, speaking, and walking in a free way.


## Love of thinking as love for the human being

It is thinking that makes a person an independent and free being. All human dignity is based on this independence. To love a person means to love and support above all else their ability to think—their ability to think better and better, ever more independently and creatively. All good education tries to promote independent creative thinking in order to enable the young people, for the whole of their lives, to have their own thoughts about the phenomena of the world. Freedom of action is inseparable from freedom in thinking. A person is unfree when they are completely dependent on the thoughts, instruction, expert knowledge of someone else, because they cannot evaluate the other's thoughts through their own. A free person is one who has discernment in all spheres of life, including discernment about the thinking and actions of experts.

One who knows how to value and support the power of thought slumbering in every human being, will love thinking as a mother loves her child. Full of hope, they see in every adult someone who can become like a child again by giving their mind a new birth. Nature does indeed give each of us the ability to become more and more creative in our thinking, but it is wary of simply bestowing creative thinking on us, because if it did, it would deprive us of the most beautiful task of our freedom.

The question of whether man is free or not is therefore posed quite wrongly. Man *can become* ever more free through his inner development, but he does not have to. The thinking given by nature and which is dependent on the forces of heredity, cannot be at the same time a free human attainment. And the thinking that may be attained only in freedom cannot already be given by nature. Man wants to experience for himself the possibility of thinking ever more vividly and creatively, because only in this way does he produce the reality of his own freedom himself.

To deny human freedom one would have to be able to prove that the further development of thinking through its own effort is not possible. But seen scientifically, wanting to prove that something is impossible is itself an impossibility, is logically a complete contradiction. Just as proof that something is possible is not proof that it actually is, so proof that something has not been realized is not proof that it is impossible for it to be so. It is possible for a child to become an adult, but it does not have to happen; and from the fact that a child is not an adult, it does not follow that it is impossible for it to become one.

Nature gives us a merely receptive thinking which with a high degree of automaticity converts sensory perceptions into ideas, into lifeless pictures. The purpose of these dead reflected pictures in consciousness is nothing less than human freedom. Only because nature-given thinking in itself creates dead reflections, do human beings have the possibility to bring more and more life into their thinking through their own free activity. One who achieves this will experience that nothing is more important in the world than the capacity to think, for all further development towards inner freedom, and therefore to acting out of love, depends on it. Without freedom there is no moral responsibility, without responsibility there is no morality, no good and no bad. Those who recognize the moral weight of thinking will dedicate all their love to promoting thinking in every human being.

To love a human being means to see in them the creative spirit which by virtue of their thinking can deal with people and the world with ever more insight and responsibility. Truly loving a person means having limitless trust in their power of thought, in that divine spark in them which holds in itself infinite potential for development. Every person wants to be loved in their ability to discern, they will strive to promote this in themself, to expand and deepen it in all directions. To do this, they must regard individual thinking as the highest moral good, as the most sacred thing in every human being.

Significant in this respect is the narrative in the Gospel of John where, when being questioned, Christ refers to the ability of his listeners to judge what he is saying. The high priest asks him what he has been teaching the people. Christ replies that he spoke openly to the world, to mature adults, and the high priest should ask those who had heard him, because they knew what he had said. Then one of the servants slaps him in the face, a man who only experiences himself as a receiver and executor of the thoughts and orders of others. Christ says to him that he should judge for himself, with his own thinking, whether his words were helping people in the given situation or not.

Many researchers may find it difficult to regard their scientifically trained thinking as only the first level of thinking, a thinking which they still owe in large measure to nature and which can serve as the basis for the next step, for living, free thinking. They need only look around them to see what this thinking, given by nature and which only understands the sensory world, has hitherto produced: a cold world inimical if not actually threatening to humanity. Natural thinking has produced a *science* that ignores the inner being of humanity and threatens to destroy its environment. Thinking that must be freely accomplished has the task of producing a *spiritual science*, a science of the human being as a free, creative mind and spirit. And what lies within the scope of human freedom can only be attained if we *love* it with all our strength.

There is barely any art that can give us so much satisfaction as the art of thinking. The most beautiful thing in a person's life is their beautiful thoughts. Many may object here that we can find more happiness in love than in thinking, that warm feelings are more likely to make us happy than 'pale' thoughts. But we can ask: What would be left of love if we took away thoughts? Nothing would be left! Loving someone means having *recognized* much that is lovable in them, and this recognition is due to thinking. The more clearly we recognize the qualities worthy of love in an individual, the stronger and more lasting will be our experience of love also. Many people look for love as a pleasant feeling without paying much attention to their thinking in the process, and then they are surprised, disillusioned and baffled when their love seems to grow increasingly empty and lukewarm. This is hardly surprising since love as a feeling always comes as a gift, as a bonus to love for thinking.

Love is not so much the strength to do great things but rather the strength to perform even the smallest act with inner greatness. And a person's inner greatness lies in the depth and breadth of their thoughts. Loving a person means having the steadfast conviction that there is in every individual a wellspring of moral imagination from which original, unique creations can arise without cease—thoughts by which all things in the world can be recognized in their deepest essence and meaning, moral ideas by which every person knows what they have to do in the world and in what way they can enrich humanity and the world.

If a Goethe had had no ideas to bring to expression in his *Faust*, what use would all the beauty of the German language have been to him? What good would all his paper and ink have been? Goethe's works are like a great stage on which wonderful creative ideas meet, intuitions of genius, countless thoughts that plunge into all the secrets of life and seek to illuminate them from the most varied aspects. And at the end, what are an almost endearing Mephisto and a transfigured Gretchen, whom Faust after his death receives in heaven with open arms, other than immortal thought creations of Goethe's spirit?

No one is in a position to create with their thoughts the world of stones, plants, animals, and humankind, far less to realize them externally. This creation is the work of beings whose power of thought far surpasses that of human thinking. Such beings could only have given humanity the capacity to think in order to be able to repeat in a human way their joy in creating the world. Today's overwhelming materialism overlooks the role of thought and fails to recognize its value entirely. It no longer seems to know that the source of all external reality is always the thought that takes its first shape in the word and its visible form in actions. Quartz, the tulip and giraffe were thought up by the creators of the world. The wheel, the chariot, mills and clocks, were created by human thoughts! What would the world be without the inventions of human thought? How can anyone say that forming thoughts about things is a waste of time?

Is not the thought of the wheel, without which today's world would truly look very different, not something to be wondered at? A person's life is as beautiful or otherwise as their thoughts, is as entertaining or boring according to what is going on in their thinking. Thinking is the highest form of love, and insight into a thing is the deepest witness of love to it. When thinking grasps something in its deepest essence, the human being becomes one with the thing. A maxim in the Aristotelian-Thomistic school of thought says: The knower in his thinking activity, and the thing known in the process of being known, are one—also numerically one! Thinking is the suspension of all alienation between human being and world, between person and person; it is the most perfect form of love, for what does love mean other than becoming one with the beloved.

A good, promising thought about my present situation in life gives me joy, it gives me the strength I need to move forward on my life's path. Even the deepest abysses can be crossed with the right thought. If the chasm I see before me is terrible, even if a veritable mouth of hell opens up in front of me and my situation seems desperate, my thoughts can always save me. It is in them I can find the strength never to give up. Thinking is the richest wellspring of strength in life. With thinking I can overcome the greatest obstacles.


## Love for speaking and love for walking

In Goethe's *Fairy Tale* of the green snake and the beautiful lily, there is the question 'What is more lively than light?' to which the answer is 'Conversation'. In contrast to the animals, human beings can speak; through speech they can communicate their thoughts and this results in an exchange of thought between individuals. What moves a person inwardly in their soul is carried outward on the wings of words. Another person grasps with their thinking the thoughts that are contained in the spoken words, understands the meaning of what the other wishes to say, and the separation between person and person is removed. Through speech, through conversation, the uniform light of thinking becomes, as it were, the many-hued world of colour. Thinking is put into speech with a different nuance of colour by each person.

The magical Greek word *logos* means both *logical* thinking as well as the word by which the thought is expressed. Humanity was seen as the creation of the divine Logos, of the Divine Thought that comes to utterance in the world and through the world. Humanity itself is capable of thought and speech, is capable of becoming ever more creative in its thinking, ever more eloquent in the expression of its thoughts through the word. No wonder then that in the Gospel of St John the being that cherishes the purest and most profound love for all human beings, that human-and-divine being who loves the faculty of thought and speech in all people above all, is called the Logos. This being gives every human being the power to produce creative thoughts which, flowing from the ground of the world, grasp the world's meaning and love the world's goal. From this being, people learn the art of speaking words of love that can fill the heart with enthusiasm.

Nature is the expression, the language, of the divine Spirit. The Spirit speaks to us in every stone, every plant, every animal. It is up to us to learn to understand this language of the creative Spirit ever better. The world is never mute for one who knows how to listen to it; it speaks continuously, in loving words that express the inner essence of things— also of human beings—in thoughts that are comprehensible for the one it loves. People utter in words for their fellow human beings what they think, feel, and will. Parzival too had to travel a long road before he was able to *utter* the important question concerning the ailment of Amfortas. Every question evokes an answer, it longs for the word that comes back from the other and allows both people to experience community in thinking.

What does the solitary thinker gain through speech? What is added to mute thoughts by conversation? The thoughts of others! I gain these in addition to my own thoughts when I converse with another. Through conversation (the Platonic dialogues are an archetype in this respect) we get an intimation of how immeasurable, how utterly inexhaustible cosmic reason is when even in its particular reflection in the thinking of each human individual it is inexhaustible.

Individual thinking serves our understanding of the world; conversation serves the communication between us. In conversation, people agree that the world is inexhaustible, that the thinking of an individual can only ever grasp certain points of view. Each of us can think correct thoughts, and each of us can only benefit by adding to our own thoughts the thoughts of others. In thinking we can experience the unity of the world; in speaking, the manifold nature of its possible expression. The world is a work of art truly to be marvelled at; it is an infinite wealth of crystallized thoughts, and every human being is a totally unique reflection of this infinity.

In speech people do not only express their thoughts but also their intended actions, their will-impulses, ideals and life goals pushing towards realization in the external world—that which is not only spoken but also done, wishing to be put into deed. At the end of a conversation when everything has been said, the people get up and *go off* in different directions, each to their own specific place where their activity is waiting for them. Each person takes their own path, on their own two legs and feet, and in their own individual way.

The first thing the child masters, before it learns to speak and think, is walking upright. Where does this first love of the child come from, the striving into uprightness, whence the indescribable joy the child expresses when it is able to take its first steps without help or outer support?

Walking independently is the first step into freedom, into free mobility in space and time. A train *carries* many people to a common destination, but then they all get out and each one starts *walking*. Each one directs their steps according to their business, each one knows in their head exactly where they have to go and what they have to do. And people are happier when they can walk under their 'own steam' than when they are driven. The paths a person covers in their life, the countless steps they take, bear the stamp of their unique individuality. It is quite impossible for two people to take exactly the same path, or even to take it in the same way.

Thinking and walking represent a wonderful polarity that is balanced out in speech, since we can speak about both what we think and what we do. People look for agreement in thinking, for what is universal, for the truth that applies to everyone. But everyone walks their own individual path because the ways of destiny we must all tread are unique, because the contribution each of us must make through our actions is unique. Walking, the movement of the lower limbs, is the prerequisite of action: our feet carry us to where our hands have something to accomplish, where we have to carry out for our fellow human beings deeds and actions for which only we have the necessary gifts. Like the paths a person walks, a person's acts are completely unique too. To love a person in their distinct individuality means to pave the way for them that they want to go, the way they must go in order to use their very individual gifts for the good of all people through their deeds, to fulfil a task for humanity that only they can fulfil.

# Love for one person, love for all people

When love wants to be more than just self-indulgence, when it tries to make the concerns of the other its own, it will endeavour to understand ever better what the individual in humanity is for humanity, and what humanity is for the individual. One who loves another will take seriously what they need from the other for their own existence, but will also further everything this other can give their fellow human beings. And loving all humanity as a living supersensory organism, means understanding ever better the thousand paths by which all individuals and all nations are integrated in each other in order to help each other progress. What is needed most urgently in humanity today are people who carry all of humankind as a single organism in their thinking awareness, have it so present in their mind that this love can become a source of inspiration in even the smallest everyday act.

To love a person means to love above all that second person in them that consists of pure love for others and has always known its life-task. It is the artist of their life who directs every step of their upright gait to where they have something to do for their fellow human beings. Every person bears an invisible twin inside them. In all of us there is a selfish I that thinks primarily about itself, and a loving I that lives by love for all people. I cannot love the person with whom I have to deal here and now without thinking of the people to which they belong, to all humanity in its many-layered ramifications, in its common struggle. And it is of little use to me or others if I indulge in a love for all humankind in general without taking care of the individual who, in their need, is knocking right now on my door.

In our twofold love for the human being—for the individual and for the whole of humanity—the free development of the individual is loved for the sake of universal brotherhood, for the sake of what only the individual in their uniqueness can bring into humanity as a whole; and solidarity that encompasses all people is loved for the sake of freedom of the individual, as the necessary foundation for individual development and the free activity of every person. Loving humanity for the sake of the individual, and the individual for the sake of humanity—in struggling to achieve a balance in this twofold love, human beings experience the warmth of heart that flows into our head and limbs, that gives light to our thoughts and strength to our deeds.

Twofold love for human beings is like the love for the twofold world in which human beings live, the world of spirit and the world of matter. For, man is the work of art arising from the mutual love between spirit and matter, he is the being in the world in which spirit and matter move each other forward in a thousand ways. Love of spirit becomes human when spirit is loved for the sake of matter, because matter without love is empty, incapable of filling the human heart. And love of all material things only becomes beneficial when all matter is loved for the sake of the spirit, as the arena for the becoming-human of spirit, as the only place where the deeds of love can become human flesh and blood.

Those who despise the world of matter deprive the spirit of the possibility of becoming flesh and of being able to work as spirit in man. Those who fail to recognize the spirit or disregard it, rob the material world of its sheen, of its true beauty. We might say that the one-sided spiritualist is one who values spirit and spurns matter, and the one-sided materialist is one who acknowledges matter and regards spirit with contempt. But looked at more deeply, it is the one-sided spiritualist who disdains spirit the most, because they disembody it, deprive it of its humanity; and the one-sided materialist fails above all to recognize matter, because they do not see the spiritual treasure it bears in its maternal lap.


## Love as the balance between freedom and brotherhood

Society as an organism is the embodiment of human love. The three fundamental forces of love—love for freedom of the individual, love for the solidarity of all people amongst themselves, and the love for the human being in every person—come to expression in the social order's threefold structure. They are the three spheres of life that only the genius of love can recognize and appreciate in each sphere's particular quality and in their mutual dependencies.

The first of these spheres encompasses all economic activity that involves producing the goods and services necessary for the physical existence of all, and circulating them for the consumption of all. Economies thrive on a very particular form of love which we can call the art of *solidarity* or brotherhood. For the satisfaction of pure needs, the modern economy is structured above all on the division of labour, and division of labour means that everyone is dependent on the work of others:  no one can work just for themselves, they can only work in association with others. The natural law of the economy is mutual love, mutual help. Only by internalizing this attitude in the heart of each individual can our economic processes be designed harmoniously and humanely. In the economy, love means that people provide each other with all the tools each one needs in order to devote themself as a gifted and free individuality to their creative mind, their artistic activities, their budding abilities, so as to use these for others. Through mutual help it becomes possible for each person to satisfy all their needs—for food, drink, clothing, education, health care, housing and so on.

A second independent branch of societal life arises from another and very particular kind of love: namely, by the legitimate desire of each individual person, in the production of goods and services, to use their skills freely. In the love for free, individually designed creation, everyone should find their own field of activity, because only they can know what skills they have and how these can best be used for the benefit of people in general. This branch includes the cultivation of culture, scientific research, education and upbringing of children, the promotion of all talents, all artistic activity, and the religious treatment of the world of spirit. The driving force in this sphere is love for *freedom* in the sense of the free initiative of every person in how they deal with their own talents and skills.

The love of solidarity and the love of freedom can only be experienced as tense opposites. But the concerns of freedom and those of solidarity must always be striving towards each other in order to stay healthy. Those who work one-sidedly for individual freedom, the freedom fighter—which is in the blood of every entrepreneur, and everyone is an entrepreneur in many respects—will tend to disregard solidarity between people. Because the free creative activity of the individual is indispensable for the health of the social organism, a person can 'fall in love' with this creativity to such an extent that they overlook how individual freedom, without the basis of economic solidarity, just hangs in the air, as it were, and can do nothing. On the other hand, those who stress the need for mutual help, for brotherhood—which primarily includes the classic worker, and who is not in many respects a 'worker'?—have a tendency to grant too little value to the free development of the gifts of the individual, without which, however, no mutual help is possible.

Because individual freedom and collective solidarity must always create a healthy tension, life requires that there be a constant mediation between these two opposites. This mediation is provided by a third kind of human love, through a balancing love that understands how to attribute equal value to both freedom and solidarity. It is the love for the dignity of all people as human beings in so far as they are all givers alike through their gifts, and all receivers alike through their needs. This third sphere of society, which deals with justice, equal rights and duties for everyone, can only thrive if it is separate and independent because it is essential that it does not become alienated from either the one-sided spirit of freedom or from the spirit of brotherhood. It must draw its inspiration solely from the spirit of complete *equality* of all people in their dignity as human beings, and always attempt to attribute *equal* weight to freedom and brotherhood.

Economic life puts love for the needy person in the foreground, whereas the actively creative life puts love for the gifted person there. In legal life there is love for the equal and equally worthy individual in every human being. To the extent that every individual is as equally a human being as every other, and with equal dignity, we all have the same rights and duties towards each other. We have the same right to receive all the solidarity and help we need for our free creativity, and, in using our abilities and through our solidarity, we have the same duty to enable the free activity of all others. Solidarity with all people is love's most sacred duty; the individual free activity for all people, is its highest right.


## Love as ideal realism

The wisdom and healing power of love becomes concrete and has direct effect when two people meet. Each of us has people whom we encounter only rarely or irregularly, and others whom we encounter regularly or even engage with daily, which strengthens our mutual influence on each other. The words *encounter* and *relationship* express a difference in the way we meet or are with each other in the love between two people. The word *encounter* points to a juxtaposition of two worlds that in a certain sense stand opposite one another—two people, each of whom follows their own very individual path in their thinking and emotions, as well as in the goals of their will and in their deeds. By contrast, the word *rela-tionship* points to a mutual force of attraction, to a deeper interweaving of two souls, each of which feels more or less drawn and bound to the other. An encounter can be very external and perhaps only a one-time event. A relationship on the other hand arises from repeated encounters in which we get to know each other better and better, and the love that deepens in this way strengthens the attraction and makes it evident that we find a stimulus in the other for our own further development.

Because in every encounter and in every relationship two worlds meet that on the one hand are related, yet on the other are different, the basic exercise of love is to promote the related element on the one hand, and to perceive and acknowledge the different element on the other. The art of societal life, the pursuit of a balance between freedom and solidarity, is exercised most diligently by love in every daily encounter, in every daily relationship. Here love becomes the concrete realism of life. Love feels responsible for the shaping of our relationships with other people. It knows that love will only have a future in the totality of humanity if there are enough people who exercise the art of love again and again in a friendship, a marriage, a family, or a business.

The polarity between encounter and relationship, between being juxtaposed to one another and being drawn to one another, shows us the twofold mission of love: to give the other person freedom with respect to the development of their completely individual abilities, but then, by contrast, also to help them in meeting their needs which are far less individual than their talents. Love's moral fantasy not only knows that it must love a person's talents very differently from their needs, but also endeavours to find the concrete *how* in every encounter and relationship. It therefore tries to establish the right balance between love for the freedom of the other and care for their particular needs in the here and now. A person wishing to live in freedom feels truly loved when the other is able to leave them alone and really give them free space. At another time, the same person would want to be loved in a completely different way, they would want the person who loves them to help them fulfil their needs.

When someone on the street asks the way, they know exactly when the information is enough. As long as they feel they know too little, they will experience all further information as helping love. As soon as they feel they've got what they need to know, they may feel any more words to be holding them up, as hampering their freedom. Thus we can experience that the transition from needing to having flips over in an instant. As long as we still lack something, we feel in need, but the moment we have everything, the centre of our focus turns to the task waiting to be fulfilled and for which we now feel we have everything we require. As clearly as we can distinguish between love that helps and love that leaves us free, so we can just as clearly experience the opposite, depending on whether we experience ourselves in a situation of needing or of having.

In the daily relationship between two people, judging this 'right moment' when the one turns into the other, can become much more complicated—the moment when well-meant help begins to be a nuisance or when, vice versa, my 'making myself thin' becomes 'too thin' for the other. The same person who has just poured out their heart, obviously looking for comfort, may want to be left alone half an hour later. And my partner, who told me to go to hell ten minutes ago, now insists that I drive them to the station. Only love knows what is too much or too little in each case. If you need the help of a friend who is good at composing a text, but you know they are going through a difficult time, it is not easy to judge whether they would be glad to be asked to help or whether they would rather be left alone. It is not the cool rational mind that will be able to sense this, only love.

For a small child, helping nurturing love is like air to breathe; for a teenager going through puberty, the same nurturing love is like poison. Here only a love that leaves them alone is helpful, a love that has the strength to trust in the freedom of the loved person and in the positive forces that everyone carries inside in their own way. True love is so flexible in its actions that it can always act differently depending on the situation. It can just as well intervene as hold back, depending on what is good for the other. Genuine love is as inventive in its thinking as it is flexible in its actions. Loving means above all wanting to understand the other, because only out of a recognition of the other's deeper nature can we see when they are asking for help and when not.

The purest expression of love in the immediate actuality of everyday life is the *love of action*, the love for what we, in the creative development of our own self, have to do here and now, for this alone can really meet the needs of others. It is a facet of the wisdom of love, with which humanity was created, that the gifts of all people in their entirety correspond to all their needs. No human being at the present stage of development can fully discern how the use of their abilities benefits *all* human beings, or how the gifts of *all* human beings serve to satisfy that person's own needs. But love can do what thinking consciousness is not yet able to do; the loving heart can have intimations of things the head does not yet understand. Thus the reverse side of love for what one has to do can only be a profound *trust* in the capacity for love in every human being, in their ability to become in their inner self, through the creative love for their deeds, ever more what they can be for all others.

A pure love for action frees us from any desire for some kind of 'success' in the action. In the wish for success, self-development becomes a means to an end, and we do not feel free but biased. But if a person experiences their self-fulfilment in the carrying out of each deed and with presence of mind in love, they will be able to feel one with other people at the same time. For, self-fulfilment through love for what we have to do and for what we are doing at this moment, is the highest form of love for our own self, and at the same time is the deepest proof of love for all other people. Love for the deed is pure love for the self *because* it is love for the other, and it is pure love for the other *because* it is love for one's own self. Here self-realization is experienced as the deepest form of love for the other.

Love works with a stroke of genius when the one that loves is able, through the intuition of their heart, to help the loved one to deeper self-knowledge than they could have reached alone. In what is reflected back to us by a loving person, our own image can appear in all its purity and beauty, freed from the opaque haze of selfishness. Many who love know the abilities of their loved one better than the loved one does themself. The deeper meaning and highest joy of love is experienced when, in the eyes of the one who loves, there appears the pure image of the beloved's better I. Thus a person may show their everyday self to another in the hope of finding the reflection of their loving higher self in the eyes of the lover.

The more purely love carries the image of the beloved in its heart, the less it will try to exert an influence on the other's will. Every human being can only progress in their love and freedom by exploring everything possible or even impossible. We become free only through our own life experience, and the deepest form of love is love that does everything it can to enable this. How eloquent the image suddenly becomes of the loving father in the Gospel parable, who endows his younger son with his possessions and then releases him to gain his own experience in life!

## Love as real idealism

Love for *one* person gradually extends to love for the *many* individuals who are connected with them; and the love for many people can find no rest until it becomes love for *all* people. In the age of a world economy and globalization, of globe-encompassing information networks and world finance, all people have more and more to do with each other. The connectedness of all people, their mutual dependence, the common fate of the earth and humanity, can be experienced more and more directly.

A mother's love for her five-year-old child deepens more and more the better she gets to know her child and is aware what is and isn't good for it. She will be aware that the quality of the food she feeds her child is linked in multiple ways to the world economy, beginning with price and going on to the question of how much the forces of nature in the food have been changed by humans—through genetic manipulation, for example—with unforeseeable consequences for the health of her child.

It is not possible to really love a person without knowing their nature, and a real knowledge of human nature is in turn not possible without also bringing into consciousness the profound connection of all people with each other and with nature. To love someone means to love all those on whom the satisfaction of all the loved one's needs and the appreciation of all their abilities depend. In a globalized world economy, this means all people, without exception. In order to know and love a human being, one must recognize the whole of humanity ever better, ever more deeply, for this is the living organism to which the beloved belongs. The health of their body depends directly on the health of the world economy. Whether they themself can love or are loved, also depends on the state of love in humanity as a whole. And the free, completely individual unfolding of their abilities and how they use them, depends on how much the economic and legal life in humanity in its entirety knows how to value the freedom of the individual.

Love becomes truly idealistic in its striving to recognize ever more deeply and more comprehensively the whole of humanity as a unified organism, and when it is also able to understand even better our own task and that of others in this organism. Individual states and nations are becoming increasingly powerless in their role as mediator between the individual and the whole of humanity. The twofold love for the individual and for the whole of humanity is not something that can be prescribed by the state or enforced by law. Whether it is a matter of the health system, work regulations or retirement provision, the state must increasingly refer to the responsibility and free decision-making of the individual.

Only the individual person can think and love, never a group or a nation, which after all consists only of individual people. Only the individual can decide to love every human being and all humanity—no state is capable of this. Only an individual can act; a group has neither hands nor feet. Every national economy is becoming increasingly impotent over against the world economy, but the individual human being is becoming more and more powerful. We can make decisions—for example about the way we deal with our money, where and how we use our purchasing power,—which have a direct influence on the world economy and at the same time can directly express our love for humankind and nature.

The highest ideal of the human being is the divine Imagination of love which has created humanity as a living, ensouled organism, and every individual human being as a vital cell, as an indispensable member, in this organism. The essence of the human being is their love for all humankind in which and by which they live, and the essence of humanity is the love for every individual person through whom it is kept alive. The two arts of love—support for the individual and requirement for community—find their necessary counterforce in two varieties of egotism. The one kind of egotism wants to love a person without caring for those whom the person loves and by whose love the person lives. But love for humanity can also be egotistical if it stays abstract and fails to become real towards the person actually standing before me. Then it remains pure self-gratification, spiritual lust, another form of self-love.

We are mistaken if we want to *be* someone who loves humanity without actually *becoming* so anew in each encounter we have with the person before us here and now. In the encounter with an individual person, egotism is overcome by love for the whole of humanity; and in the relationship with the whole of humanity, it is overcome by love for the person standing opposite me 'in the flesh'. At the highest level of its moral imagination, love is the recognition of the individual in their identity within the whole, and the rediscovery of the whole of humanity in each individual.

The love of all the beings of nature for man is not free, but, as already indicated, completely 'natural', because nature, out of itself, has no possibility of denying man its love. It is created as pure love for man: all the stones, plants, and animals have served man's process of becoming human since time immemorial. Love for man is the meaning of nature, and our becoming-human can only take place in gratitude for the love of all nature's creatures for man. Man, on the other hand, is free to refuse nature his love; he can also refrain from repaying love with love to his mother the earth. And what does a loving mother do if she finds no reciprocal love? She can do nothing but love more. Natural catastrophes are not the revenge of nature against human beings who do not love her, but loving admonitions by spiritual beings seeking to shake us awake, who always want only good for humanity. The earth stays faithful in its love for human beings; but human beings can become unfaithful to the earth and destroy themselves.

There is only *one* environment for everyone just as there is only *one* humanity for all people. It is the nature of love to strive for a balance between the satisfaction of humanity's common needs and the development of the gifts in all people. Only love's intuition can find the balance between the common right to mutual help in a globalized economy and the right of the individual to develop their gifts freely.

When I consume or use something others have made, I can experience my love in gratitude to that fact; when I make something myself or provide a service for others, love finds its expression in my creativity. One who loves is grateful in receiving and imaginative in giving. And love is an unceasing giving and receiving on all levels of existence and among all living beings; it is the law of the mutual relations between all the individual beings of this earth. The meaning of the earth is love for man, because everything in visible creation is created for the sake of man. All the imperatives of nature find their meaning and perfection in man's striving for freedom and love.

The love for all human beings shines out ever more brightly the more clearly each individual recognizes the collective destiny of all; the more the individual human being makes the fate of humanity the dearest concern of their heart, the warmer love becomes. The Being who is full of love, the Christ, feels so united with every human being, feels such deep compassion for the suffering of all people, that the fundamental principle of His love is, 'What you do to the least of these my brothers and sisters, you do to me also.' This principle of perfect love is the highest ideal for the development of every person. People are connected in such a way that anything done to one person is not without influence on all others. What is done for one person is done for all. The globalized economy is only the external evidence that all people are of one spirit, one soul and one body.

The social organism is threefold in its striving for *freedom* in the development of individual gifts, for *brotherhood* in the satisfaction of the needs of all, and for *equality* in respect of mutual rights and duties. Love is also threefold: it is love for the freedom of the individual, love for support in community, and love for the human dignity in each person.

The first social ideal of love is production of goods and services spanning all humanity, focused not on profits but on service to the consumer. It is production that draws its inspiration from the needs of all the people of the world. In a world economy, all manufacturing can only be based on what is needed by all consumers the world over. The needs of the whole of humanity must therefore be perceived more and more comprehensively, recognized better and more lovingly, so that worldwide production can be directed in such a way that it serves all people equally.

The second social ideal of love is the freedom of the individual human spirit. The unified spirit of humanity manifests itself in the special gifts of separate individuals. Love for the human spirit is a love that gives free rein, a love that is open to the surprises with which each new generation wishes to fructify and enrich humanity with its new discoveries and talents. The creative imagination of the nations and of individual human beings is fed from the common wellspring of the spirit of humanity's moral fantasy, the essence of love itself. This spirit is both unity and infinite diversity, individualizing in freedom, and at the same time generating brotherhood in reciprocity.

The third social ideal of love is the pursuit of an international law that recognizes as its highest goal the equality of all nations and of all people. Every nation has the right to self-determination only if this right includes the duty to grant every other nation the same right and to enable its fulfilment. Every individual has the right to the satisfaction of their needs and to the free exercise of their abilities only if they grant the same right to every other person and do everything within the scope of their power to ensure every person can attain to this right as a human being.

Love for the body of humanity, for its needs, is expressed in a globalized economy. Love for the soul of humanity is expressed in the pursuit of international law, of a justice that encompasses all people and recognizes the equal dignity of all people as human beings. Love for the spirit of humanity lights up in creative thinking and in the free creative work of each human individual.

Through centuries of development, love's moral fantasy liberates all selfishness into love for all people, it transforms all antipathy into sympathy for all beings, and dissolves all lovelessness like the sun dissolving fog into light and warmth.

# A note from the publisher

For more than a quarter of a century, **Temple Lodge Publishing** has made available new thought, ideas and research in the field of spiritual science.

Anthroposophy, as founded by Rudolf Steiner (1861-1925), is commonly known today through its practical applications, principally in education (Steiner-Waldorf schools) and agriculture (biodynamic food and wine). But behind this outer activity stands the core discipline of spiritual science, which continues to be developed and updated. True science can never be static and anthroposophy is living knowledge.

Our list features some of the best contemporary spiritual-scientific work available today, as well as introductory titles. So, visit us online at **www.templelodge.com** and join our emailing list for news on new titles.

If you feel like supporting our work, you can do so by buying our books or making a direct donation (we are a non-profit/ charitable organisation).

office@templelodge.com

 **TEMPLE LODGE**

*For the finest books of Science and Spirit*